Office in a Minute

Steps for Performing Basic Tasks in Microsoft Office 2010

Diane L. Martin

First Edition

My PC Associate NYC

244 Fifth Avenue, Suite 2337

New York, NY 10001

www.mypcassociate.com

Office in a Minute

Steps for Performing Basic Tasks in Microsoft Office 2010

Diane L. Martin

My PC Associate NYC

DISCLAIMER

While My PC Associate NYC takes great care to ensure the accuracy and quality of these materials. All material is provided without any warranty whatsoever, including but not limited to, the implied warranties of merchantability or fitness for a particular purpose.

ACKNOWLEDGEMENTS

The author gratefully acknowledges the support and encouragement of Judy Ganeles Wilson, LaToya Trowers Bell, Sharon Cunningham, Francine Martin and Rajasekhar Vangapaty.

Table of Contents

Part I Microsoft *Word*

Part 2 Microsoft Excel

Part 3 Microsoft PowerPoint

Part 4 Microsoft OneNote

Collect the Entire

Office in a Minute Series

www.mypcassociate.com

www.amazon.com

www.createspace.com

About the Author

Diane Martin is executive director of My PC Associate NYC. She has been teaching computer applications in the fields of business and higher education since 1981. In 1999, with a background in business and legal technology, Diane migrated to the field of higher education, becoming the director of computer networking and support for a college of business and technology in New York City. She subsequently taught Computer Applications for Business at the DeVry Institute of Technology, and the Laboratory Institute of Merchandising, both in New York City. She is currently on the faculty of Continuing Education at Long Island University. Diane is a member of the Association of Information Technology Professionals and the Association of Women in Computing.

In addition to a Juris Doctor degree, Diane also holds a Master of Science degree in Instructional Technology from New York Institute of Technology, and a Bachelor of Arts degree in Liberal Arts from Long Island University. She is a certified Senior Professional in Human Resources, (SPHR) a certified Microsoft Office Specialist, and she holds a New York State Business School Teacher license.

About this Book

The purpose of this book is to serve as a quick tutorial for those who are largely unfamiliar with Microsoft Office (Home and Student Edition) features, functions and benefits. If you want to learn the most basic steps of this wonderful suite of software applications, you have come to the right place. Through the quick tutorials, you will learn how to create, manage and save documents in Microsoft Word. You will also become acquainted with how to use Excel to create a simple spreadsheet. We will introduce you to Microsoft PowerPoint, and explain how you can use this application to create professional-looking presentations. Finally, we will introduce you to the Microsoft OneNote application. Here you will become familiar with how to use OneNote to organize all kinds of data like documents, photographs, videos, notes, and a whole lot more.

To facilitate learning we have liberally employed the use of screen shots, arrows, and handy notes pages. Finally, we have included the estimated time it should take you to complete all of the tasks within a given chapter. Most basic tasks can be completed in four to five steps and in less than two minutes.

You will learn so much more as you work with Microsoft Office. What we really attempt to do here is to provide you with systematic instructions for performing basic tasks that will help you become a productive user. For this reason, individuals who have been working for a year or more with the Microsoft suite will likely require instruction that is more advanced.

To those of you, who are relatively new to MS-Office, welcome to our tutorial. Keep in mind that proficiency comes with practice. As you continue to work with these applications, your confidence, productivity and skill will improve.

Happy Computing!

D. Martin

Dedication

To my niece Justine,

Anything is possible, if you believe.

My Notes:

"I think it's fair to say that personal computers have become the most empowering tool we've ever created. They're tools of communication, they're tools of creativity, and they can be shaped by their user."
Bill Gates

Chapter 1

GETTING STARTED WITH MICROSOFT WORD

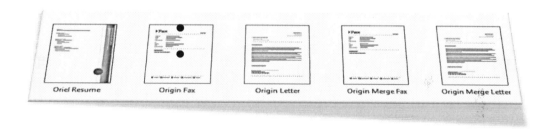

- *Launch Microsoft Word*
- *Identify Screen Elements*
- *Select and Edit Text*
- *Save a Document*
- *Close an Existing Document*
- *Open an Existing Document*
- *Create a New Document*

🕐 *The Estimated Time to Complete These Tasks is 15 Minutes.*

Launching the Microsoft Word Application

Open the Microsoft Word application installed on your computer by clicking on the Office Start button. You will find this button located in the lower left-hand corner of your desktop. Locate the Microsoft Word icon and then double-click your mouse button; this will launch the application.

The Microsoft Word Environment

Figure 1

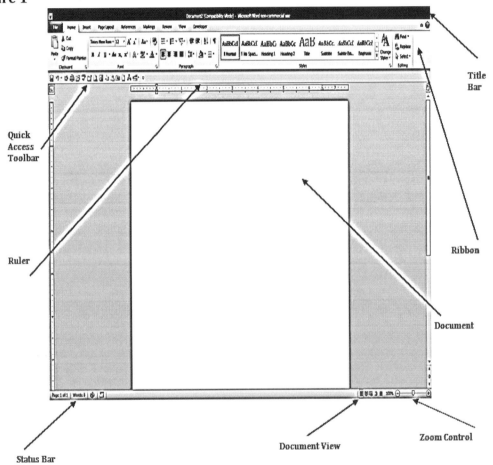

Take a few minutes to become familiar with the screen elements depicted in Figure 1. The Microsoft Word application opens with nine tabs respectively named File, Home, Insert, Page Layout, References, Mailings, Review, View and Developer. Each tab has a ribbon organized into groups. For example, look at the Home tab, and notice the buttons within the Font group. This group contains buttons related to changing the appearance of text, and allows you to apply bold, underline or italics to basic text.

Selecting and Editing Text

After Microsoft Word opens to a brand new document, you may simply begin typing; however, if you hope to become proficient, you should understand a little more about the fundamentals of text editing in Microsoft Word.

Observe that as you type, a cursor (|) like this one shifts to the right with each keystroke. Move your mouse around a bit, and you will likely see this (I). This is your insertion pointer.

Figure 2

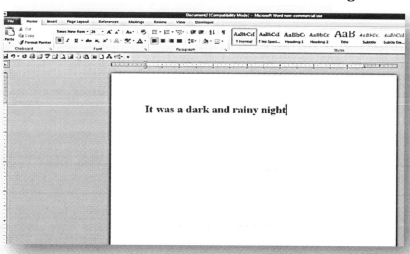

The act of merely typing your text is straightforward; however, when it comes to editing what you have typed, managing insertion pointer will be invaluable. For example, suppose you want to edit the text depicted in Figure 2.

Start by typing the words "It was a dark and rainy night." If you decide to change the word rainy to stormy, you have several options. You can place your cursor at the end of the line and hit the backspace key 11 times to delete all of the characters up to the word "and", or you can click your mouse anywhere within the word rainy and double-click your left mouse button. When you double-click on the word **rainy,** it becomes highlighted. Now type the word stormy. Whenever you want to change or edit text in Word, you must first select that text by moving your mouse over the text and then double-clicking your left mouse button.

> **Note**: All Mouse click instructions assume readers are right-handed. Mouse orientation can be modified in the Windows control panel.

To Select Text

1. Hover with your mouse over the desired text.

2. Double-click your left mouse button.

3. Locate and press the delete key on your keyboard or type alternative text.

Saving a Document

1. Click on the File tab.

2. Select the Save menu option.

3. Type a name for your document.

4. Click on the Save button.

Close an Existing Document

When you are finished working on your document, simply click on the File tab and then choose the Close icon located near the top of the menu. If you have not already saved your file, you will be prompted to do so. Click on the Yes button if you want to save your changes.

Figure 3

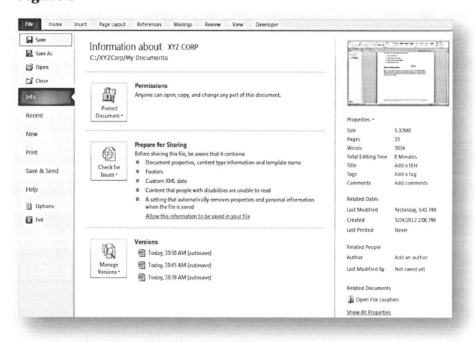

Opening an Existing Document

An existing document is one that has previously been saved to your hard disk, flash drive or floppy drive. You can click on the File tab to access Word's Backstage View, and then you can select the Open button. Alternatively, you can select the Recent menu option to view a list of recently opened files. See Figure 4 below.

To Open an Existing Document

1. Click on the File tab.

2. Click on the Open or Recent menu option.

3. Select the desired file.

4. Click on the Open button.

Figure 4

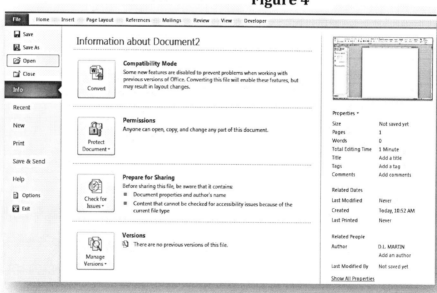

Other useful menu options include Save and Send. This feature will allow you to both save and e-mail a copy of your document. The document can be sent as an attachment or can be printed within the e-mail message form.

As you become more comfortable with Word, try exploring the Options menu. Through this menu, you can customize the Word environment.

Creating a New Document

Select the File tab to initiate the opening of a new document. From the Backstage View you are provided with a variety of new document options. Word also comes with a variety of templates designed to help you quickly prepare the most common types of documents. See Chapter 4 to learn more about Microsoft Word templates.

To Create a New Blank Document

1. Select the File tab.
2. Click on the New menu option.
3. Select the Blank document icon.
4. Click on the Create button

Figure 5

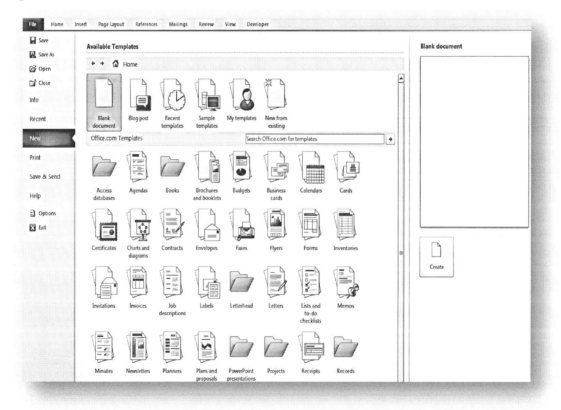

Chapter 2

FORMATTING A DOCUMENT

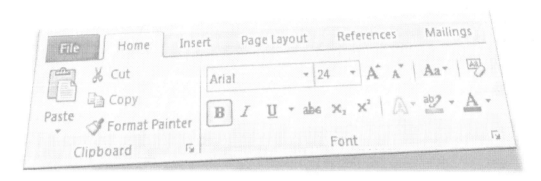

- *Apply Character Formatting*
- *Apply a New Font*
- *Use the Format Painter*
- *Align Text*
- *Use Bullets & Numbering*
- *Apply Styles*
- *Clear Character Formatting*
- *Undo the Last Command*
- *Insert a Header or Footer*
- *Use Page Layout Features*

The Estimated Time to Complete These Tasks is 12 Minutes.

Applying Character Formatting

Focus your reader's attention by applying Microsoft Word's character formatting features. With one button and in less than two seconds, you can apply **bold**, underline, *italicize*, **color** or change the typeface of the selected text.

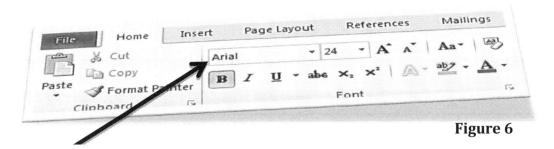

Figure 6

To Apply Character Formatting

1. Click on the Home tab.

2. Click into the desired text and then double-click to select the text.

3. Click on the Bold, Italics or Underline button.

You can change the appearance of text by experimenting with various types of fonts. Word makes this very fast and easy to accomplish. Furthermore, the Word application comes with more than two-dozen serif and sans serif fonts. A serif font or typeface has little edges or feet (serifs) on each letter. Notice the letters in this paragraph. Contrast them with the word "**Paragraph**". We applied the **Arial** font to the word. Arial is an example of a sans serif. The letters have no edges or feet, in fact, the word sans means "without. " Generally, serifs are easier on the eye. Many books are written with a serif typeface; however, the font you choose will largely depend on your taste and needs. Remember one of the most efficient ways to edit text, is to first select or highlight that text, and then apply formatting options. Here is the quickest method for applying a new font to your text.

To Apply a New Font

1. Select the text to be formatted.

2. Click on the Home tab.

3. Click on the Font drop down box and choose the desired font.

4. Click on the Font Size button if you also wish to change font size.

Save Time with Format Painter

Word's Format Painter feature can be a real time-saver. Imagine that you have applied bold and italics formatting to one paragraph, and wish to apply both formats to another part of your document or another word in your document. Format Painter allows you to copy the character formatting of a single word and then apply it to another word, sentence or paragraph.

To Use Format Painter

1. Click on the word that contains the desired formatting.

2. Click on the Format Painter to copy the formatting.

3. Select the desired text to apply the formatting.

Aligning Text

The Microsoft Word program makes four basic text alignment options available: left, centered, right, or justified. See the Paragraph group on the Home tab in Figure 7. To center text on the page, you will want to do the following:

1. Select the text you want centered.

2. Click on the Center Button or press (Ctrl + E).

Figure 7

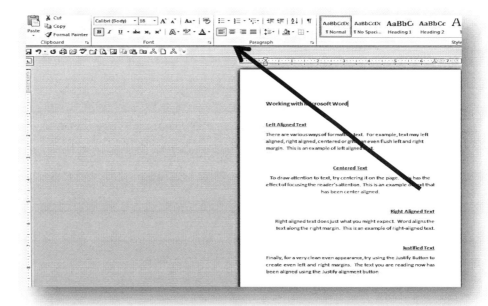

Formatting Text with Bullets and Numbering

Within the Paragraph group, which is located on the Home tab, you will find two extremely useful tools for formatting text. You can quickly enhance any list of items with bullets and numbering feature. Furthermore, like many features in Word, there are multiple ways to apply the bullets or numbering style to your text. Below is just one method.

To Format Text with Bullets

1. Click on the bullet button and begin typing the first item, and then press enter.

2. Type the next item, and repeat as many times as necessary.

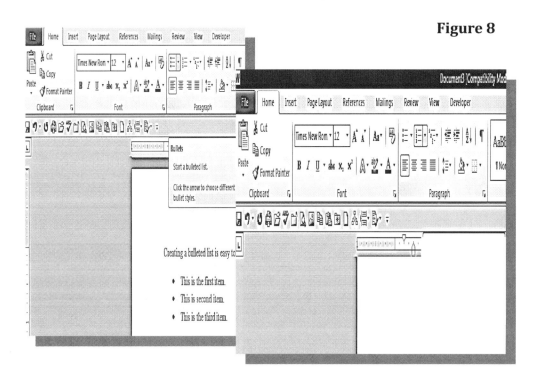

Figure 8

To view the wide variety of bullet styles that come with Microsoft Word, simply click on the Bullets dropdown box. See Figure 8 above.

Repeat the same process above to apply the numbering style. Notice too that the Numbering button also has a dropdown box with a variety of numbering styles.

Apply Styles to Basic Text and Save Time

Microsoft Word is chock-full of timesaving features. For example, so far you have learned how to apply character formatting to your text. However, Word's built in Styles feature takes formatting even further, by providing you with preformatted headings, titles and subtitles. See Figure 9. In addition, Word allows you to create and save your own custom formatting for use not just in your current document, but in other documents as well. Think of styles as preformatting. Examine the Styles group located on the Home tab.

Figure 9

The style **Heading 1** is made up of the Arial Font is **bold** and has a 17-point font size. You can change the appearance of a title, subtitle or heading by selecting the text and then selecting one of the available Heading styles. Using Styles can save you the steps it normally takes to select a font, a character format and font size.

To Apply a Heading Style

1. Click on the Home tab.

2. Select the desired text.

3. Click on the desired heading style.

To Clear Character Formatting

If you change your mind, simply click on the clear formatting button.
This will erase any formatting such as bold or underline from the selected text.

Undo Your Last Command

Note, that you can also undo your last keystrokes by clicking the Undo button. You will find this button located on the Quick Access Toolbar. Use it once and you will be hooked.

Inserting a Header

A header contains text that is repeated at the top of each successive page within a document.

1. Click on the Insert tab.

2. Click on the Header button.

3. Choose the desired header style.

4. Type the text you wish to appear on each page.

5. Click on the Close Header & Footer button.

Figure 10

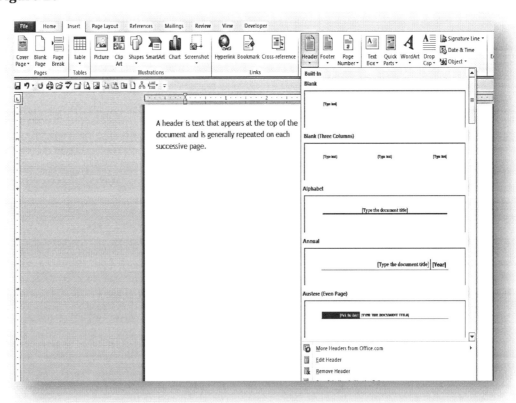

Note: When the Headers dropdown box is opened, a Headers & Footers Tools tab appears. See Figure 10 above. If you do not want the header to appear on the first page of your document, select the Different First Page button.

Inserting a Footer

Footers contain text, which repeats at the bottom of each successive page.   To place a footer within your document, you will want to do the following:

1. Click on the Insert tab.

2. Click on the Footer button.

3. Choose the desired footer style.

4. Type the text you wish to appear at the bottom of each page.

5. Click on the Close Header & Footer button.

Figure 11

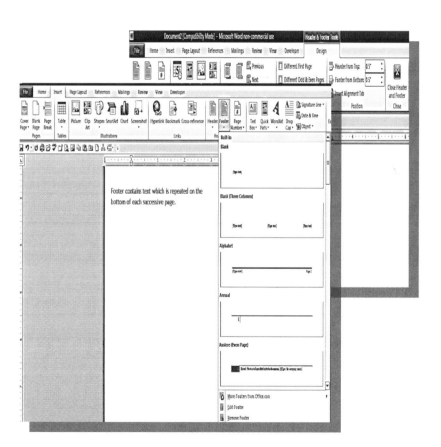

Notice that when the Footers dropdown box is opened, a Headers & Footers Tools tab appears. See Figure 11 above. If you do not want the footer to appear on the first page of your document, select the Different First Page button.

Working with the Page Layout Feature

Word makes it possible for you to control the layout of your document. If you want to change the orientation of your document from portrait to landscape, or you want to change your margin settings, you will want to become acquainted with Word's Page Layout tab. Think of the Page Layout tab as mission control where you have a variety of page management tools available in one dialog box. See Figure 12 below.

To Change Margin Settings

1. Select the Page Layout tab.

2. Click on the Page Setup dropdown box.

3. Type your margin settings.

4. Click on the OK button to save your settings.

Figure 12

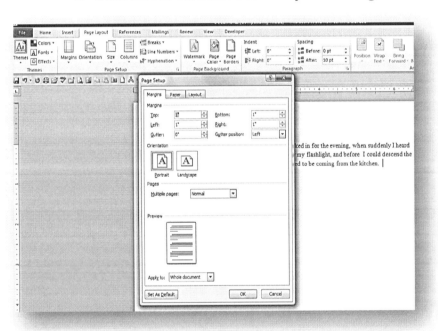

If you choose the Set As Default button, Word will apply your margin settings to all newly created documents. This same rule will apply to page orientation. Although we will not discuss it in detail here, you should know that Word gives you the option of applying settings to the whole document, or from the location of your cursor forward.

Chapter 3

✂ SHORTCUTS & UTILITIES

- *Use Shortcut Keys*

- *Use Cut, Copy and Paste Buttons*

- *Check Spelling & Grammar*

- *Print a Document*

- *Customize the Quick Access Menu*

- *Use the Mail Merge Feature*

🕑 *The Estimated Time to Complete These Tasks is <u>25</u> Minutes exclusive of Mail Merge.*

The Cut, Copy and Paste Feature

Often you will want to copy text from one location in your text to another. Alternatively, you can permanently move text to another part of your document. Word's Copy, Cut, and Paste feature allows you to do this in mere seconds. The copied text is moved to the Clipboard. Think of the Clipboard as that magical place where data temporarily waits until you decide where to place it. There is more than one-way to copy and/or move text in Word. For example, if you want to copy text do the following:

1. Click on the Home tab.

2. Select the text you want to copy.

3. Click on the Copy button.

4. Place your mouse where you want the copied text to appear.

5. Right click your mouse button and then choose Paste.

To Remove or Cut Text

1. Select the text you want to cut.

2. Click on the Cut (scissors icon).

Short -Cut Keys

If you find yourself sitting in the cramped seat of a plane, train or automobile without enough space for an external mouse, try using these short-cut keystrokes. Whatever you copy is moved temporarily to Word's Clipboard. Just select the data, choose copy, and then place your cursor where you want to paste it. Press Ctrl + V and it is done!

• Copy	Ctrl + C
• Paste	Ctrl + V
• Cut	Ctrl + X

The Spelling & Grammar Feature

Microsoft Word contains a spelling and grammar-checking feature that will automatically check your document for common spelling errors. In addition, you can quickly spell check a word by selecting it, then clicking on the Spell Check button. Be advised that proper nouns, and words typed in all capitals will generally **not** be reviewed.

1. Click on Word's Review tab.

2.   Click on the Spelling & Grammar button.

3. To accept a suggested correction, click the Change button.

Note, that Word also contains a handy thesaurus. To use the thesaurus, simply select the desired word then right click your mouse button, and choose **S**ynonyms.

- **Ignore Once**: Prompts Word to skip a word not in its dictionary.

- **Ignore All**: Prompts Word to ignore all occurrences of a word not in its dictionary.

- **AutoCorrect:** Prompts Word to check its Autocorrect entries for the correct spelling of a word.

- **Options**: Opens the Proofing dialog box within the Options menu and allows you to modify default spelling and grammar settings.

Printing a Document

There are several ways to initiate the printing of a Microsoft Word document. As you become more comfortable with Word, you can experiment with various methods. However, if you are new to MS-Word, we recommend that you initiate printing from the File tab. See Figure 13, and examine the Print menu dialog box.

To Print a Document

1. Select the File tab.
2. Click on the Print menu option to open the Printer dialog box.
3. To print the entire document, click on the Print button
4. To print selected pages, click on the settings button and enter the print range, i.e. 1-3.

Figure 13

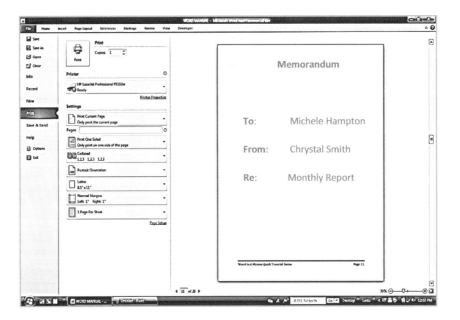

In addition to printing your document to a printer, you can also print to OneNote. OneNote is a Microsoft application that comes with MS-Office. Think of OneNote as an electronic notebook. If you do not have an immediate need for a hardcopy, OneNote may be a good place to store a digital copy of your document.

Customizing Your Quick Access Toolbar

Place commands where you can quickly access them by customizing the Quick Access Toolbar. You can find the Quick Access Toolbar just below the ribbons on each Microsoft Word tab. See Figure 14.

To Customize the Quick Access Toolbar

1. Select the File menu.
2. Click on the Options menu.
3. Choose Quick Access Toolbar.
4. Choose the desired command from the Popular Commands dropdown box.
5. Click on the Add>> button.
6. Choose the OK button.

Figure 14

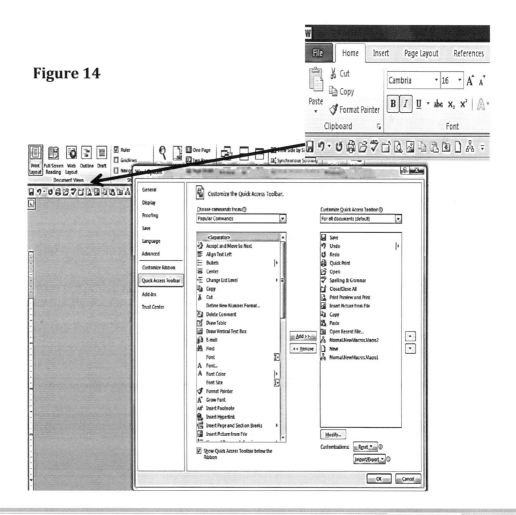

My Notes:

Chapter 4

WORKING WITH VISUALS

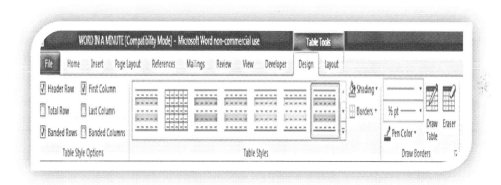

- *Create a Table*

- *Use the Table Styles Gallery*

- *Insert an Illustration into a Document*

- *Adjust or Size an Illustration*

- *Use SmartArt*

- *Place Shapes into your Document*

🕐 *The Estimated Time to Complete These Tasks is 11 Minutes.*

Working with Microsoft Word Tables

When you want to organize information, there is no better tool than a Microsoft Word table. A Word table can make it extremely easy to type and edit text. Fortunately, with a little forethought, you can put together a very polished and professional looking table. Moreover, Word comes with a gallery of styles for your table, and actually allows you to try them on before you apply them to your data.

See Figure 15, and observe how this table consists of three columns and three rows. In addition, the table also contains banded rows of alternate colors. Together these elements make up the Light Shading, Accent 5 Table Style. To create a table in Word you must select the Table dropdown box, located on the Insert tab.

To Create a Table

1. Select the Insert tab.

2. Click on the Tables dropdown box.

3. Click on the Insert Tables menu option.

4. Enter the desired number of rows and columns for your table.

5. Click on the OK button.

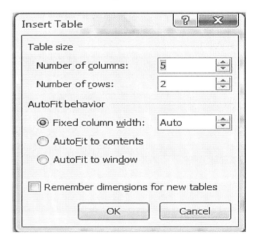

Figure 15

Column 1	Column 2	Column3

Make That Table Look Great!

The Design Ribbon

Enhance the way your table looks by using the Table Styles feature. When you double-click anywhere within your table, the Design ribbon appears. Simply click on the Design tab, and then choose the desired table design from the Table Styles Gallery. See Figure 16. To try-on the various table styles hover with your mouse over each style option.

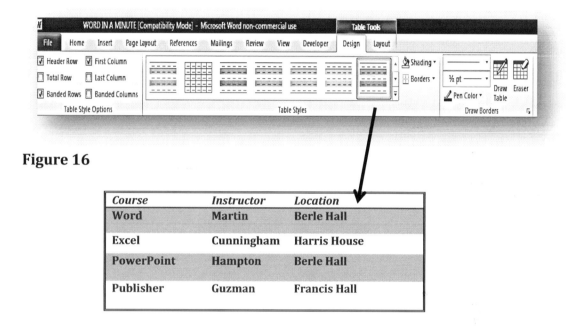

Figure 16

Course	Instructor	Location
Word	Martin	Berle Hall
Excel	Cunningham	Harris House
PowerPoint	Hampton	Berle Hall
Publisher	Guzman	Francis Hall

The Layout Ribbon

If you double-click within your table, Word also activates the Table Tools tab and the Layout ribbon becomes active. From this tab, you can choose to insert additional rows and columns. In addition, there is a Sort button, located in the Data group. This feature is a wonderful and essential feature if you want to arrange data in ascending or descending order.

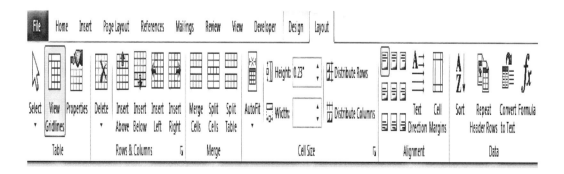

Placing a Picture into your Presentation

Pictures really do help tell your story, and fortunately, Word makes the placement of pictures and other media types within a document very easy to do. Clip Art contains a gallery of illustrations, videos, photographs and audio files that come bundled with Word.

In general, personal photographs are stored in your My Pictures folder. Therefore, if you want to insert the photograph you took of your dog Fido, choose the Picture button located on the Insert tab. On the other hand, if you are looking for some illustrations to spice up your PTA flyer you will want to open the Clip Art gallery. Place your cursor in your document where you want the picture, photograph, video or audio file to appear, and then perform the following steps:

1. Click on the Insert tab.

2. Select the Clip Art or Picture button.

3. Type a category name, (*for Clip Art only*).

4. Click on the Go button.

5. Click on the desired image.

Adjust the Size of Your Photographs or Clip Art

After you select your photograph or Clip Art, Word places it into your document surrounded by handles. See the dog graphic in Figure 17.

To make the image larger or smaller, simply hover with your mouse over any of the handles, and notice the double arrow. When the double arrow appears, hold down your left mouse button to size the image. To delete a picture click on it, and when the handles appear, press the delete key on your keyboard.

Figure 17

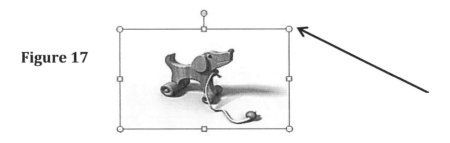

Opened Clip Art Gallery

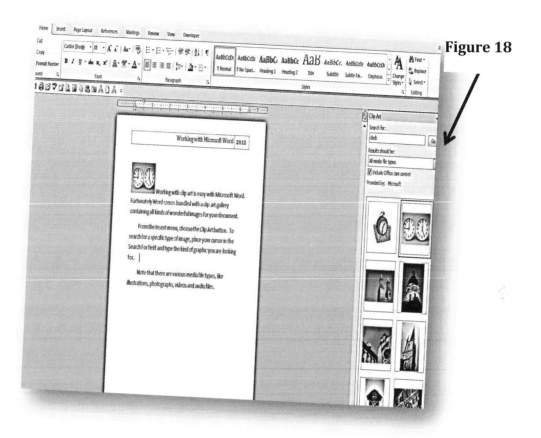

Figure 18

If you are looking for a particular type of graphic, type its name in the Search for field within the Clip Art dialog box. See Figure 18. For example, if you type the word **clock**, the Clip Art Gallery will display a number of clock or time-related images.

You can control the types of images the Clip Art Gallery retrieves. For example, if you click on the Results should be field; you may choose to limit your search to specific media types, such as photographs, videos, illustrations and audio files.

****

Look Smarter with SmartArt

To create a visually appealing document, consider the use of Microsoft's SmartArt. The SmartArt gallery comes with more than 40 objects including organizational charts, flow charts and process symbols. See Figure 19 below. Creating an organizational chart is a common business practice. To become more acquainted with Word's SmartArt feature, try creating the organizational chart depicted in Figure 19.

To Create an Organizational Chart

1. Select the Insert tab.

2. Place your cursor where you want the chart to appear.

3. Click on the SmartArt button.

4. Click on Hierarchy within the Navigation pane.

5. Choose the desired layout.

6. Click into the placeholders and enter the names and titles of the individuals.

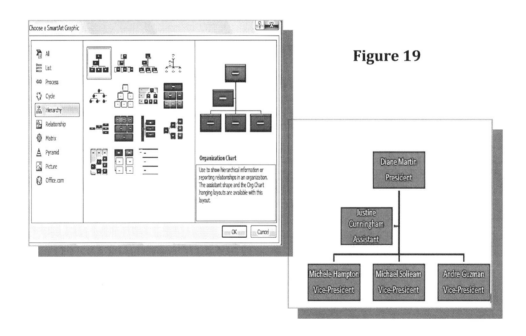

Figure 19

SmartArt Graphic Options *

<u>Lists</u>:   Select this option to create visual effects for bulleted items.

<u>Process</u>:   An option suitable for depicting routes, procedures and progression.

<u>Cycle</u>:   Represents a sequence of stages, tasks, or events in a circular flow.

<u>Hierarchy</u>:   Shows hierarchical information or reporting relationships

<u>Relationship</u>:   Depicts connections, links, or a correlation.

<u>Matrix</u>:   Used for concepts, relationships sequenced or grouped blocks of information.

<u>Pyramid</u>:   Used to show containment, proportional, or interconnected relationships.

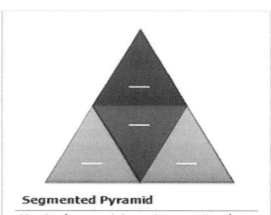

Segmented Pyramid

Use to show containment, proportional, or interconnected relationships. The first nine lines of Level 1 text appear in the triangular shapes. Unused text does not appear, but remains available if you switch layouts. Works best with Level 1 text only.

Example of a SmartArt Segmented Pyramid 1

Descriptions taken from Microsoft's Word SmartArt Gallery.

Working with Shapes

Word comes with a wonderful array of shapes you can use to enhance a document. Whether you need a rectangle, triangle, circle or star, Word likely has just what you need. You can find Shapes within the Illustrations group, located on the Insert Ribbon. See Figure 20.

To Insert a Shape

1. Place your cursor where you want the shape to appear.

2. Click on the Insert tab.

3. Click on the Shapes dropdown box.

4. Select the desired shape.

5. Hold down your left mouse button and then drag your mouse left or right to draw and size the shape.

Figure 20

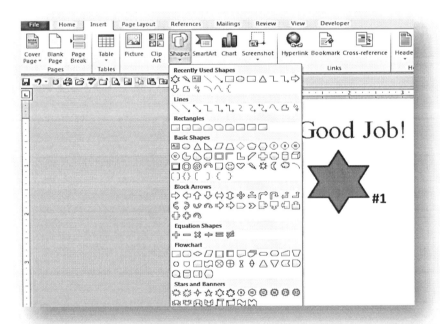

To delete a shape, click on it to select it. When the handles appear, press the delete key on your keyboard. You can use the textbox shape to place text over graphics.

Work with Templates

If you ever find yourself in need of a resume, fax cover sheet, book report or flyer, you will be pleased to learn that Microsoft Word comes bundled with a wonderful variety of pre-designed documents to kick-start start your project. You will also find these templates categorized by subject.

To Access Word Templates

1. Select the File tab.

2. Click on the New menu option.

3. Select the desired template.

4. Choose the Create button.

Figure 21

While many templates are installed on your hard-drive, additional templates may be downloaded from the Internet. If you do not see what you are looking for try the Microsoft website. There you will find an additional source of templates from both Microsoft and members of the Microsoft Office user community.

Word 2010 Templates Window with Fax "Clipboard design" template Selected

Figure 22

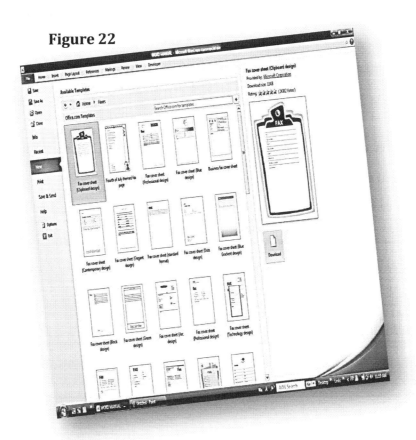

You can search for a specific template, i.e., resumes, flyers, invoices or statements by clicking into the Search Office for Templates field and typing the category name. See Figure 22 above. When you click on a template, Word displays a likeness of it for your review.

Do experiment with the different templates. In addition, do not be afraid to modify an interesting template in order to make it conform to your specific requirements.

Mail Merge

Though Mail Merge is generally considered a task for more advanced users of Microsoft Word, I thought I would share a few thoughts with those of you eager to try out this wonderful feature. If you want to send a single document to multiple people, you can save time with Word's mail merge feature. Word's built-in Wizard program will guide you through the entire process of combining a list of addressees with a letter. During this process, you are placing codes in your document that contain the information for each individual addressee. Once you have worked with merging letters, envelopes and labels will be easy to do as well.

I recommend that you create your list of addressees before you begin working with the merge feature. Using a Word table is a good way to create your list. In addition, we also recommend that you create the basic letter you want to send to the addressees first. Remember where you have stored your documents, as you will be required to locate them as part of the merge process.

Setting up a Mail Merge

1. Select the Mailings tab.

2. Click on the Start Mail Merge dropdown box.

3. Choose the Mail Merge Wizard option.

4. Select the document type or accept the default.

5. Click on the Next button and then follow the on-screen instructions.

Figure 23

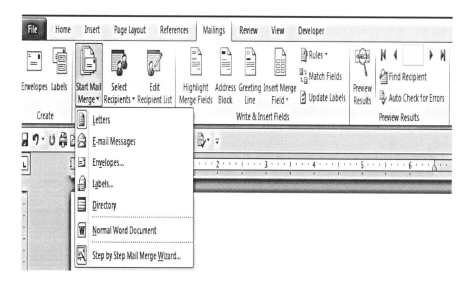

My Notes:

Chapter 5

MS-WORD RIBBONS & TABS

- *File Tab*

- *Home Tab*

- *Insert Tab*

- *Page Layout Tab*

- *References Tab*

- *Mailings Tab*

- *Review Tab*

- *View Tab*

Microsoft Word Ribbons & Tabs

The File Tab – Backstage View

Figure 24

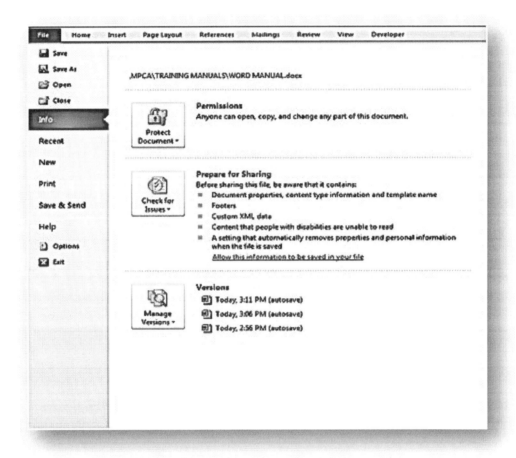

Click on the File tab in Word 2010 and Microsoft displays what it calls the Backstage View. From this tab you can save files, access recently opened files, create a new document, print or exit the Word application.

Other Word features include the ability to place security restrictions on files, and remove personal information from your Word documents.

Home

The Home tab displays a ribbon containing a host of text formatting options. Enhance documents by indenting, centering, justifying or right aligning text. Use and create styles to preserve formatted text for use in other documents or repetitively within the same document.

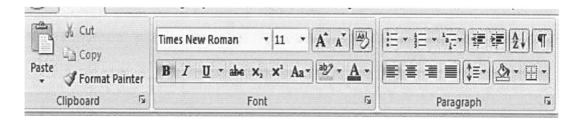

Insert

Click on the Insert tab to access features like Clip Art, Cover Page, WordArt, headers, footers and SmartArt to name a few. From this tab you can also draw shapes, create page breaks or insert a Microsoft Excel chart within your document.

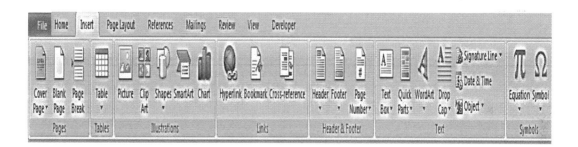

Page Layout

From this tab, you can apply colorful themes to your document, create multi-columned documents, change line spacing or place a watermark in your document. Use the Tracking dialog box to view and track changes to your document.

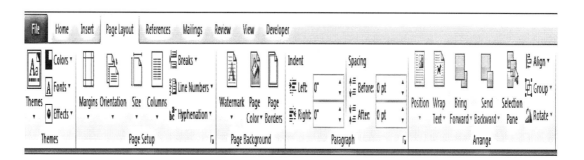

References

You will find the References tab handy for inserting footnotes, endnotes or citations into your document. This is also the site of the Table of Contents group.

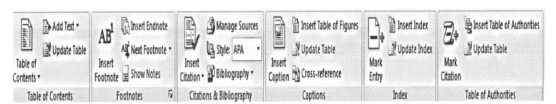

Mailings

Mail documents to multiple users easily with Word's Start Mail Merge group. To begin, type your document, and then select the Step-by-Step Mail Merge Wizard.

Review

Before you share a document with others, be sure you select the Review tab. You will find helpful features such as Spelling & Grammar, Thesaurus, and Word Count.

View

Use the Document Views, Show/Hide, Zoom and Window groups for various ways to examine and display your document.

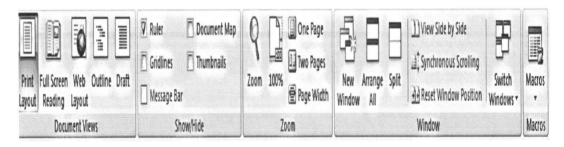

"Pure mathematics is, in its way, the poetry of logical ideas."

Albert Einstein

Chapter 6

GETTING STARTED WITH EXCEL

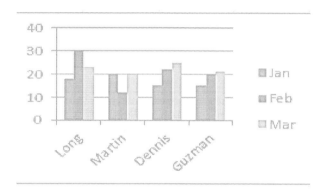

- ***Start the Excel Application***

- ***Structure and Enter Data***

- ***Work with Basic Formulas***

- ***Use the AutoSum Feature***

- ***Save a Workbook***

- ***Close a Workbook***

🕐 ***The Estimated Time to Complete These Tasks is 25 –30 Minutes.***

Starting the Microsoft Excel Application

Start the Excel Application from your desktop by clicking on the Office Start button located on your desktop. Find the Microsoft Excel application icon and then double-click your left mouse button to launch the application.

The Microsoft Excel Environment

Figure 25

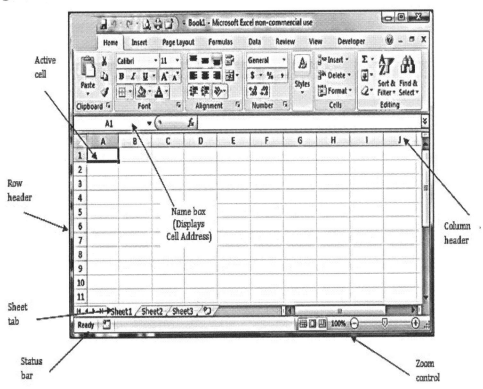

Microsoft Excel opens up to an electronic workbook with three worksheets. Each worksheet is made up of addressable cells. A cell is the intersection of a row and a column. With more than 256 columns and more than 20,000 rows per worksheet, there is more than enough room for the average garden-variety spreadsheet.

If you do need more worksheets, adding them to your workbook is a cinch. Simply click on the Insert Worksheet button. It is right next to the Sheet3 tab at the bottom of your workbook. See Figure 25.

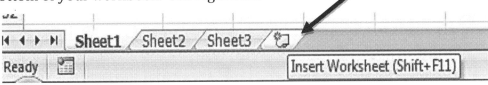

Office in a Minute

The Microsoft Excel Environment

Figure 26

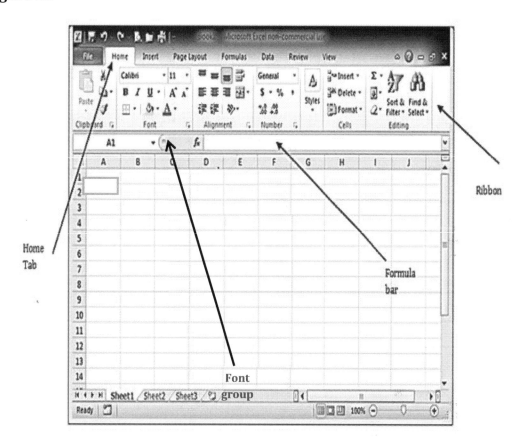

Notice the tabs at the top of the Excel window. Each tab contains a ribbon with features organized around common functions. For example, notice the Font group includes the Bold, *Italics* and <u>Underline</u> buttons.

Recall that a cell is the intersection of a row and a column, and it has an address. Thus, in the image above, the address of the highlighted or active cell is A1. This address also appears in the Name box. See Figure 26. As you will see, referring to cells by address makes it easier to change and calculate the content within those cells.

We will cover formulas a little later; however, keep in mind that a formula differs from text in that a formula must always begin with an = symbol.

Structuring and Entering Data into a Worksheet

Creating a worksheet is a little like using numbers to tell a story. For example, notice in Figure 27, that our worksheet has a title and a date. This simple structure communicates the purpose of the worksheet as well as the date it was created. Now others will understand the what, where and when of our financial story.

To enter data into your worksheet, simply click your mouse in the cell where you want to begin typing. If you type a number or letter into a cell, and then change your mind, click on the Cancel (☒) button depicted in Figure 3. Click on the Accept (☑) or enter key to confirm your entry.

Figure 27

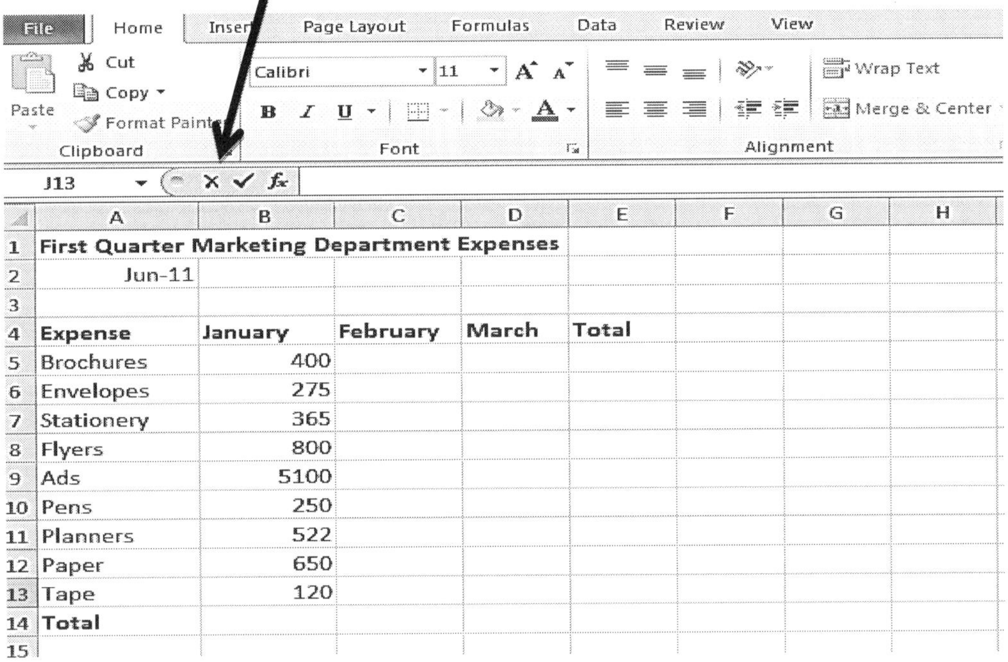

You can pull out a calculator and add the contents of our January data; however, manually calculating the data would really defeat the purpose of Excel.

A key advantage of using Excel is that it can quickly calculate data and allow us to perform what is often referred to as what-if analysis. For example, if we construct a formula that to calculate the contents of the cells B5 through B13, (in Excel terms: B5:B13) we can go back and change the numbers in any cell within that range to see how it effects our total. That is an example of what-if analysis.

Therefore, now that we have begun entering data for our worksheet, our next step will be to construct a formula that will calculate our data.

Working with Basic Formulas: SUM, AVERAGE, MIN AND MAX

Excel's built-in formulas allow you to calculate any range of numbers quickly. Remember that **all formulas must be preceded by an equal (=) sign** and follows the same scheme. For example, to add a range of numbers, such as the one depicted in Figure 28, you would click into cell B14 and type the following:
=SUM(B5:13)

To Enter a Formula into a Cell

1. Click your mouse in the cell where you want the result to appear.

2. Type an = and then type the desired formula.

3. To add a range of numbers use = **SUM(B5:B13)**

4. To calculate the average for a range use =**AVERAGE**(B5:B13)

5. To display the lowest number in a range use =**MIN**(B5:B13)

Working with AutoSum

Alternatively, you can sum a range of numbers using the AutoSum feature.
The AutoSum feature is located on the Home tab. With AutoSum, you can quickly add any range of numbers horizontally or vertically. Think of it as a shortcut that eliminates the need to type out the formula =SUM (B3:B13). See Figure 4.

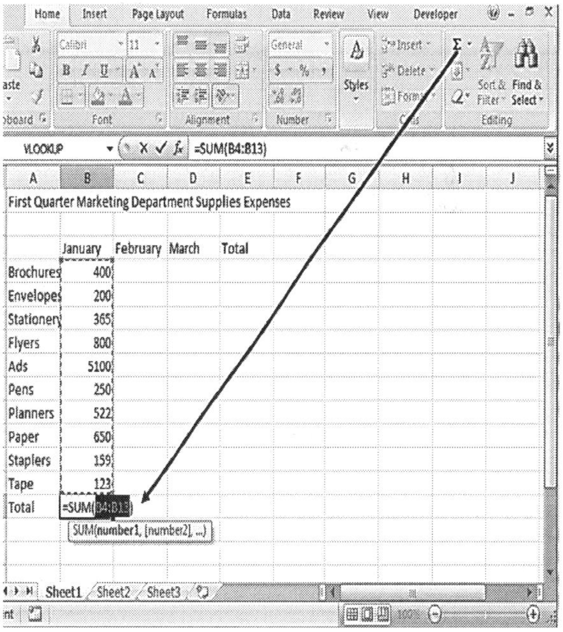

Figure 28

To Use the AutoSum Feature

1. Select the Home tab.

2. Place your cursor in the result cell.

3. Click on the AutoSum button.   (Notice the other AutoSum functions.)

4. Press the enter key to accept the selected range.

Saving a Workbook

When the Excel application is opened, your workbook exists in in your computer's random access memory, (RAM). RAM is volatile and is disrupted by power fluctuations. Therefore, until your worksheet is saved to some permanent media like a hard-drive or thumb drive you risk its complete loss. For this reason, you will want to make it a practice to save your workbook at regular intervals.

To Save a Workbook

1. Click on the File tab.

2. Choose the Save menu option.

3. Type a name for your workbook.

4. Click on the Save button.

Close an Existing Workbook

If you want to close your workbook, but remain in Excel, simply click on the File tab, and then choose the Close icon located near the top of the menu. If you did not previously save your workbook, you will be prompted to do so. Just click YES if you want to save your changes.

Figure 29

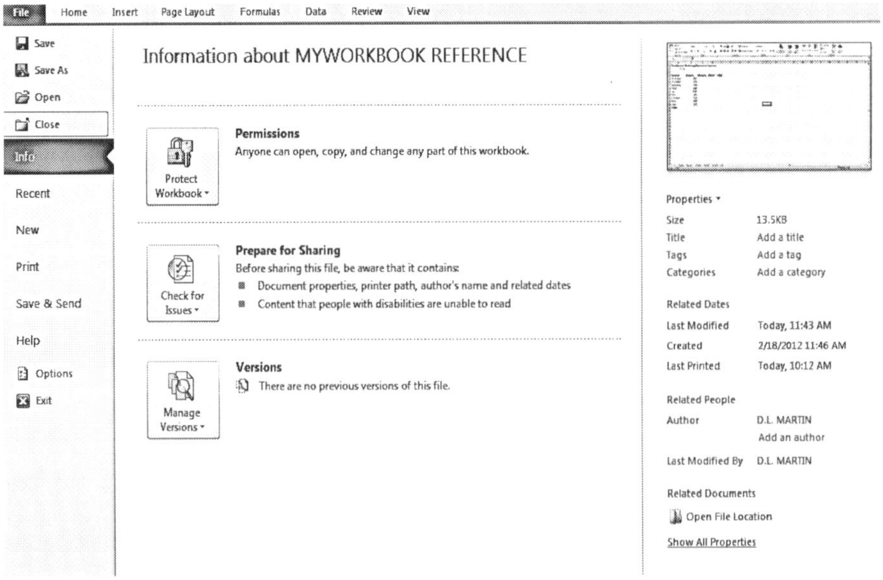

Chapter 7

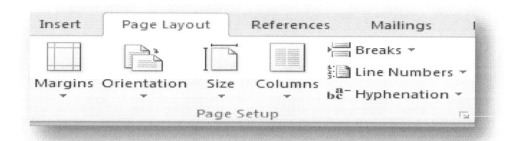

MANAGING PAGE SETUP
&
PRINTING OPTIONS

- *Print a Workbook*

- *Identify Page Layout Options*

- *Work with the Page Setup Feature*

- *Set the Worksheet Print Area*

🕐 *The Estimated Time to Complete These Tasks is 5 Minutes.*

Printing a Workbook in Excel

One of the best things about Excel is that there are several ways to initiate the printing of a workbook. For example, you can select the Print option from the File tab, or you can initiate printing using the Quick Access toolbar. Alternatively, you can also access the Print command by choosing the Page Layout tab, and then choosing the Page Setup dropdown box.

As you become more familiar with Excel, you can experiment with the various options, and then select the method you like the best. Therefore, since ribbons and tabs are so convenient, this is the route we cover in detail here.

To Print a Workbook.

1. Click on the File tab.

2. Choose the Print menu option.

3. Click on the Print button.   **Figure 30**

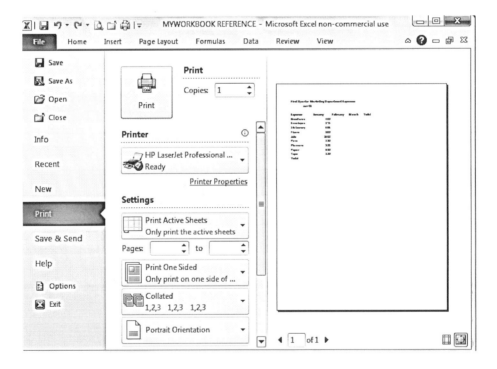

Examine Figure 30 and you will see that Excel displays a facsimile of what your worksheet will look like when printed. Notice the gridlines do not appear. In addition, there is neither a header nor footer in this worksheet. However, you can control the printing of these kinds of elements through the Page Setup feature.

Working with Page Setup Options

Excel makes it possible to manage the layout of your worksheet with a wide variety of options. For example, you can insert headers and footers into your worksheet. In addition, you can choose to display and print out your worksheet in a landscape as opposed to a portrait orientation. The row and column headers as well as the gridlines you view on the screen may also be printed in Excel.

You access these page set-up options from the Page Layout tab. See Figure 31, and notice the tiny dropdown box within the Page Setup group. When you click on this dropdown box, the Page Setup dialog box opens and displays four tabs: Page, Margins, Header/Footer and Sheet. In addition, if you click on the Print Preview button, you can see what your worksheet will look like when printed.

Figure 31

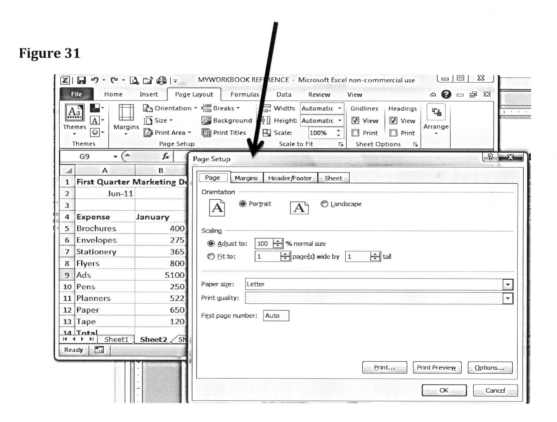

Page: From the Page tab, you can change the orientation of your worksheet from Portrait to landscape. In addition, because worksheets can grow to become quite large, they do not always print out as planned. Therefore, Excel allows you to adjust the size of your worksheet through its scaling options.

Margins: Select this tab to adjust margin settings within your worksheet.

Header/Footer: Select the Header/Footer tab to choose from a list of built-in headers and footers, or design your own by choosing the Custom Header or Custom Footer buttons. Your headers and/or footers can include pictures, the date and/or the name of your file. See Figure 32 below.

Figure 32

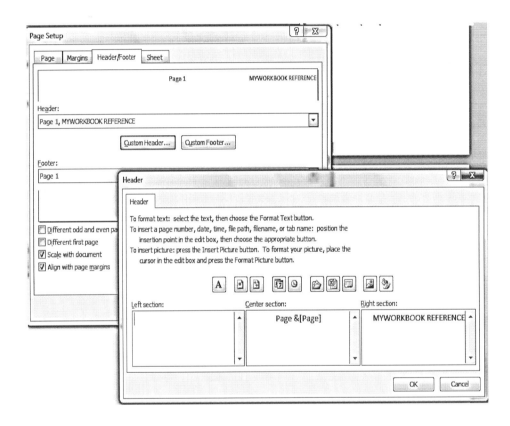

Sheet: From this tab, you can elect to print the gridlines in your worksheet. In addition, you can elect to print the familiar row and column headings that appear on screen.

You can also print a specific section of your worksheet by clicking into the Print Area box; however, I think this takes some getting used to if you are relatively new to Excel. On the next page, we will discuss another method for setting your print area.

Setting the Worksheet Print Area

You can create a print range from within your document, by selecting or highlighting the part of the worksheet, you wish to print, and then choosing Set Print Area from the Page Layout tab. See Figure 33.

Setting the Print Area

1. Drag your mouse to select the range of data to be printed.

2. Click on the Page Layout tab.

3. Click on the Print Area dropdown box.

4. Choose the Set Print Area menu option.

5. Click on the File tab and choose the Print menu option.

Figure 33

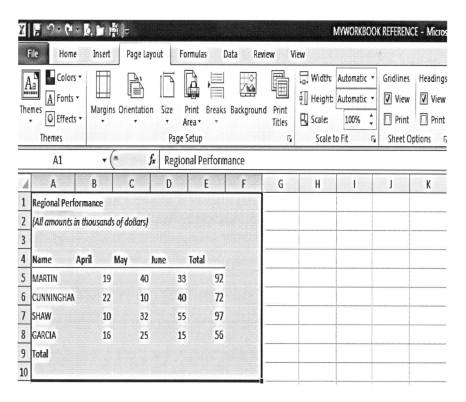

My Notes:

Chapter 8

MANAGING

&

FORMATTING WORKSHEETS

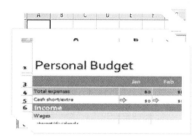

- *Format Cells*
- *Clear or Delete Cell Contents*
- *Insert Rows and Columns*
- *Apply Character Formatting*
- *Use Alignment group Buttons*
- *Use the Format Painter Feature*
- *Undo your Last Command*
- *Use the Spelling & Grammar Feature*
- *Copy Formulas*
- *Create Relative and Absolute Cell References*

☉ The Estimated Time to Complete These Tasks is 15 Minutes.

Formatting Cells

Both text and numerical data may be formatted to include dollar signs, percentage symbols, decimals and commas. Fortunately, Excel makes formatting cells very straightforward. For example, if you want to represent financial data, you will find the Number group on the Home tab quite useful. See Figure 34. **Simply select the text you wish to apply the dollar symbol to, and then click on the Currency Style button**.

 Alternatively, you can click on the Number group dropdown box; and then you may select an option from the Format Cells dialog box. See Figure 35.

Figure 34

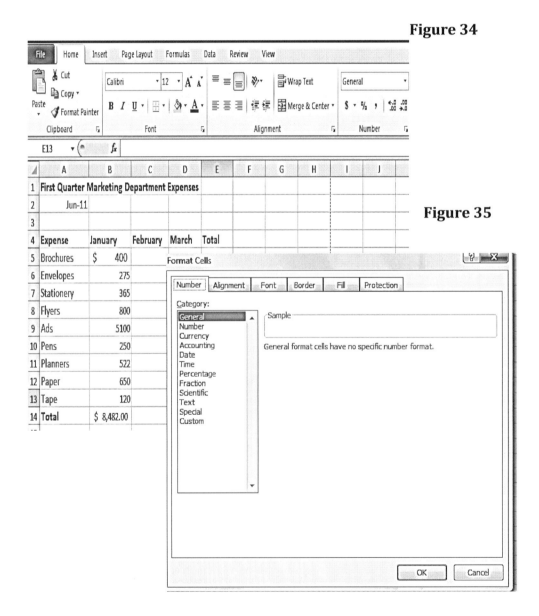

Figure 35

Deleting or Clearing the Contents of a Cell

Inevitably, you will have a need to delete some of the information you have typed into your worksheet. Fortunately, Excel has a button for that. You can choose to either clear the contents of a cell or delete the contents. See Figure 36. Note that when we click into the Total cell and press the right mouse button, a short menu is displayed.

The distinction between Delete and Clear Contents is an important one. When you choose the Clear Contents menu option, any formatting within the cell, i.e., currency symbol or percentage will remain. On the other hand, if you choose the Delete option, the formatting will be deleted along with the data within the cell.

To Clear or Delete the Contents of a Cell

1. Select the cell(s) to be cleared or deleted.

2. Right click your mouse and choose the Clear Contents or Delete.

Figure 36

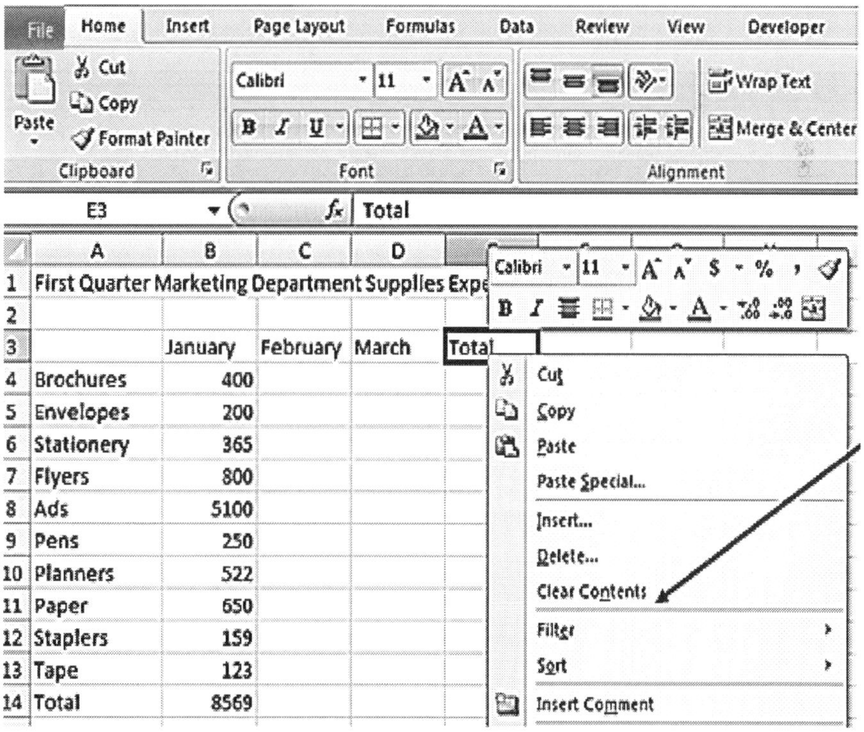

Managing Your Worksheet

Inserting Rows and Columns

Additional cells, rows and/or columns are added to a worksheet by using buttons located on the Home tab. Examine the Cells group. There you will find three key buttons: Insert Cells, Delete Cells and Format Cells. See Figure 37 and notice how the row has been selected by clicking on the row-heading button. You can follow the same process for columns.

To Insert Rows and Columns

1. Click on the desired row or column-heading button.

2. Click on the Home tab.

3. Click on the Insert dropdown box within the Cells group.

4. Select the Insert Sheet Rows button.

Repeat the steps above for <u>deleting</u> rows and columns. Observe that additional sheets can be inserted or deleted as well.

Figure 37

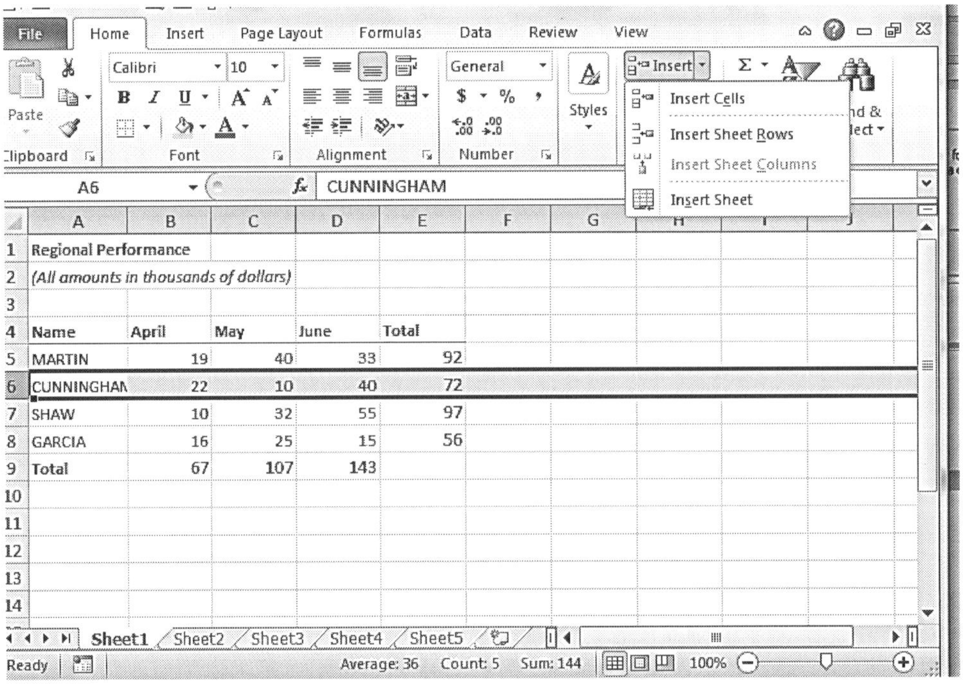

Apply Character Formatting

Focus your reader's attention by applying Microsoft Excel's text formatting features. With one keystroke and in less than three seconds, you can bold, underline, italicize, color or change the typeface.

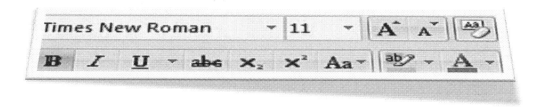

To Apply Bold, *Italicized*, or <u>Underline</u> Formatting

1. Drag your mouse to select the cell.
2. Click on the desired formatting button.

To Apply a New Font

Try changing the current font in your document to **Cambria.**

1. Select the cell to be changed.
2. Click on the Font drop down box and choose the Cambria font.
3. Click on the Font Size button if you want to change the size of the text.

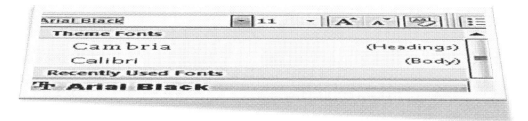

Alignment Group Buttons

Align text or numerical data within your cells by using the Alignment group buttons: Left, Center, Right and Justify. Remember to first select the cell, and then click on the desired alignment button.

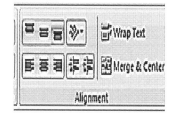

Save Time with Format Painter

If you have worked with Microsoft Word, then you already know what a time-saver the Format Painter can be. This feature allows you to copy the character formatting of a word and then apply it to another word, sentence or paragraph. This same functionality is available in Excel.

To Use the Format Painter

1. Click on the cell that contains the desired formatting.

2. Click on the Format Painter to copy the formatting.

3. Select the desired cell to apply the formatting.

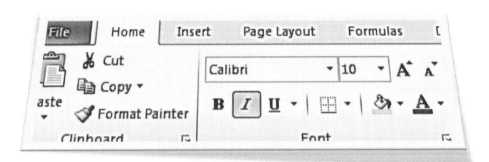

Clear Formatting

If you change your mind, and wish to remove any formatting you have applied, simply click on the clear formatting button. This will erase any formatting such as bold or underline from the selected text.

Undo Your Last Command

You can also undo your last keystrokes by clicking on Microsoft's wonderful Undo button. You will find this button located on the Quick Access Toolbar.

Spelling & Grammar

Microsoft Excel contains a spelling and grammar-checking feature that will automatically check your worksheet for common spelling and grammatical errors. In addition, you can quickly spell check a word or series of words by highlighting them and then clicking on the Spelling & Grammar Check button. Generally, proper nouns and words typed in all capitals are **not** reviewed by the Spelling feature.

1. Click on Excel's Review tab.

2. Click on the Spelling and Grammar button.

3. To accept a suggested correction, click the Accept button.

Figure 38

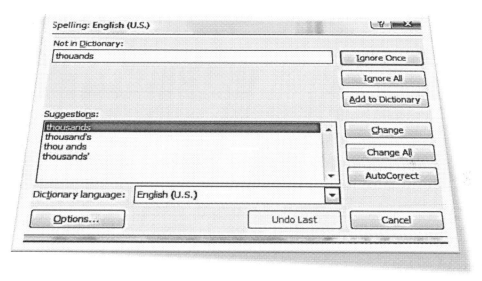

- **Ignore Once**: Prompts Excel to skip a word not in its dictionary. -

- **Ignore All**: Prompts Excel to ignore all occurrences of a word not in its dictionary.

- **AutoCorrect:** Prompts Excel to check its Autocorrect entries for the correct spelling of a word.

- **Options**: Opens the Proofing dialog box within the Options menu and allows you to change how Excel corrects and formats your text. Here you can elect to have Word review words typed in upper-case.

Managing Data

Using the Cut, Copy and Paste Feature

Often you will want to copy data from one cell to another. Alternatively, you can permanently move data from one cell to another. Excel has a Cut, Copy and Paste feature that allows you to do this in mere seconds. In fact, there are several ways to copy and/or move data in Excel.

To Copy the Contents of a Cell

1. Select the Home tab.
2. Click your mouse into the cell you want to copy.
3. Click your right mouse button and then choose Copy.
4. Click your mouse in the adjacent cell, and then click on the Paste button.
5. Press the Esc key (to halt the copy process).

Figure 39

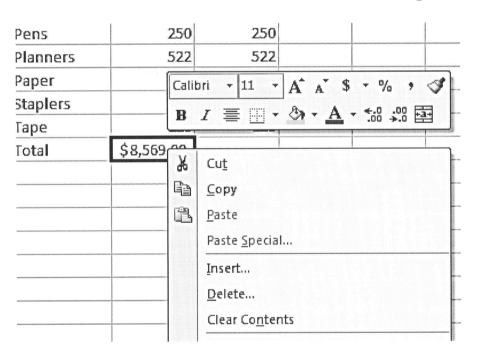

You will also find the Cut, Copy and Paste buttons conveniently located within the Clipboard group of the Home tab.

Short -Cut Keys

If you find yourself sitting in a cramped seat on a plane, train or an automobile, and you do not have enough space for an external mouse, try using these short-cut keystrokes. Whatever you copy is moved temporarily to Excel's Clipboard. Just select the data, choose copy, and then place your cursor where you want to paste it. Press Ctrl + V and it is done!

• Copy the selected text	Ctrl + C
• Paste copied text	Ctrl + V
• Cut the selected text	Ctrl + X

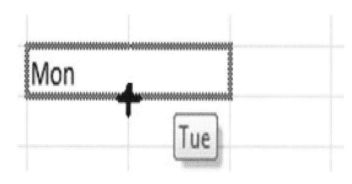

Working with the Fill Series Feature

Microsoft Excel also has a wonderful feature known as the Fill Handle. Once you have mastered using this timesaving device, you will become hooked and you will forever look for ways to put this feature to work for you. The Fill Handle can be used to fill a series of cells. For example, suppose you want to your worksheet to list the days of the week. You could type the days of the week into each of seven cells, or you could drag your mouse across seven columns and have Excel populate the cells for you.

Use the Fill Handle to Create a Series

1. Type the first word of the series, i.e. Monday.

2. Move your mouse over the lower right corner of a cell; see the crosshair.

3. Drag your mouse across the number of cells in the series.

Excel comes with a number of pre-set series like the days of the week and months of the year, but you can also create your own series.

Copying Formulas

Use the Fill Handle to copy formulas from one cell to another. For example, suppose you want to copy the formula in cell B:14 to cell C:14. Hover with your mouse over the lower right corner of the cell you want to copy; when the fill handle appears, drag your mouse to the adjacent cell.

When a formula is copied its cell address changes relative to its new location. This is what is referred to as a relative cell reference. Look at Figure 40 below, and notice the formula in B9 is =SUM (B5:B8). When copied to column C, the formula becomes =SUM (C5:C8). Many times this is the result you want. However, there will be times when you do not want a formula to change when copied.

Absolute References

Making a cell reference absolute is not difficult. All you really have to do is place a dollar sign before the row and column. For example, B5 is an example of an absolute cell reference.

Figure 40

	A	B	C	D	E
1	Regional Performance				
2	(All amounts in thouands o				
3					
4	Name	QTR. 1	QTR. 2	QTR. 3	QTR. 4
5	MARTIN	19	40	33	=SUM(B5:D5)
6	CUNNINGHAM	22	10	40	=SUM(B6:D6)
7	SHAW	10	32	55	=SUM(B7:D7)
8	GARCIA	16	25	15	=SUM(B8:D8)
9	Total	=SUM(B5:B8)	=SUM(C5:C8)	=SUM(D5:D8)	
10					

Whenever you want to view the formulas in your worksheet, select the Formulas tab, and then click on the Show Formulas button located in the Formula Auditing group.

Chapter 9

ENHANCING WORKSHEETS WITH GRAPHICS

- *Create Charts*

- *Place Illustrations within a Worksheet*

- *Use the SmartArt Feature*

- *Enhance a Worksheet with Shapes*

🕐 *The Estimated Time to Complete These Tasks is 21 Minutes.*

Creating Charts with Microsoft Excel

To make numeric data more meaningful, consider the use of a chart. Within seconds, you can use Microsoft Excel to insert any one of a variety of chart types into your worksheet. Chart types include line, bar pie and area. In fact, there are more than 40 available chart types from which to choose. First, it will be important to select the cells to be represented in your chart. See Figure 41.

1. Select the cells to be included in your chart. (**Do not highlight the total.**)

2. Click on the Insert tab.

3. Select a Chart style from the Chart group.

4. Click on the desired Chart type.

Figure 41

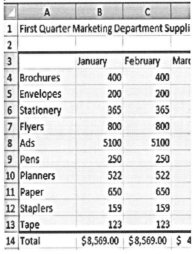

	A	B	C	
1	First Quarter Marketing Department Suppli			
2				
3		January	February	Marc
4	Brochures	400	400	
5	Envelopes	200	200	
6	Stationery	365	365	
7	Flyers	800	800	
8	Ads	5100	5100	
9	Pens	250	250	
10	Planners	522	522	
11	Paper	650	650	
12	Staplers	159	159	
13	Tape	123	123	
14	Total	$8,569.00	$8,569.00	$ 4

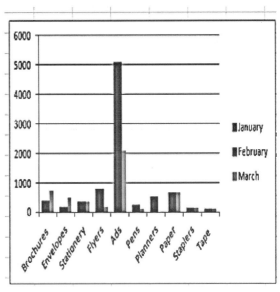

Excel Worksheet with Embedded Line Chart

If you double click on your chart, Excel will activate the chart. When this happens, a Chart Tools tab will appear. At this point, you can select an alternate chart type as well as edit the chart's data series. The chart in Figure 42 below is an example of an embedded chart.

If you want your chart to appear in a separate worksheet, just select the data range and then press the F11 key. See Figure 43 to see an example of a Chart sheet.

Figure 42

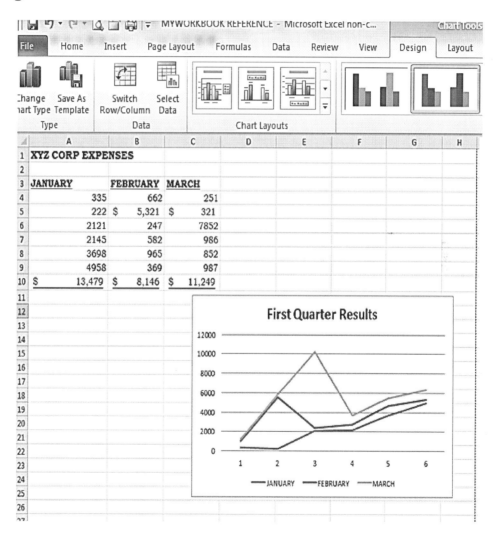

An Excel Chart Sheet – Created by the F11 Key

Figure 43

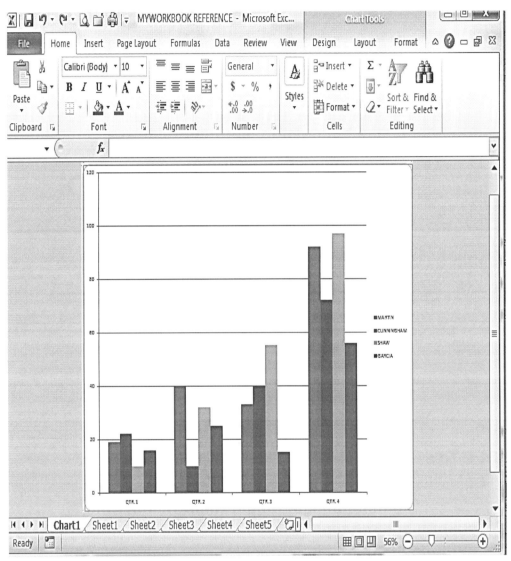

This is an example of Chart worksheet. Observe how the chart appears along side the sheet tabs in Figure 43. The chart can be renamed. If you right click your mouse button while pointing to the Chart sheet, Excel will display a short menu. Choose the Rename option, and then begin typing a new name for your chart. You can edit a Chart sheet as just you can an embedded chart. Double-clicking on the chart will activate the Chart Tools tab.

Inserting Illustrations

Pictures can be used to enhance your worksheet, and fortunately, Excel makes the placement of all kinds of illustrations, within a worksheet very simple to do. In fact, Excel comes bundled with a collection of pictures collectively referred to as Clip Art.

You may insert your own personal pictures into a worksheet or you may wish to explore and insert pictures from the Clip Art Gallery. To access your personal pictures (*usually stored in the My Pictures Folder*), select the Picture button, and then choose the Insert button. However, to open the Clip Art Gallery, simply place your cursor in your document where you want the picture to appear, and follow these steps.

Figure 44

1. Click on the Insert tab.

2. Select the Clip Art button.

3. Type the name of the desired object

4. Click on the Go button.

5. Click on the desired image.

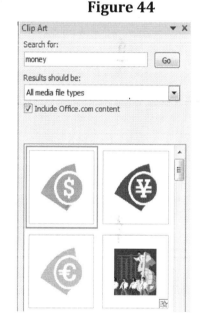

Adjusting the Size of an Illustration

After you select your photograph or clip art, Excel places it into your worksheet surrounded by handles. See Figure 45.

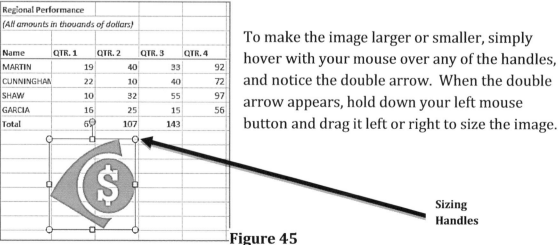

Regional Performance				
(All amounts in thousands of dollars)				
Name	QTR. 1	QTR. 2	QTR. 3	QTR. 4
MARTIN	19	40	33	92
CUNNINGHAN	22	10	40	72
SHAW	10	32	55	97
GARCIA	16	25	15	56
Total	67	107	143	

To make the image larger or smaller, simply hover with your mouse over any of the handles, and notice the double arrow. When the double arrow appears, hold down your left mouse button and drag it left or right to size the image.

Sizing Handles

Figure 45

Work with SmartArt

To create a visually appealing worksheet, consider the use of Microsoft's SmartArt. The SmartArt gallery comes with more than 40 objects including organizational charts, flow charts and process symbols. See Figure 46 below.

To Insert a SmartArt Object into a Worksheet

1. Select the Insert tab.

2. Place your cursor where you want the object to appear.

3. Click on the SmartArt button.

4. Select a SmartArt graphic, i.e., Process.

5. Choose the desired layout.

6. Click into the placeholders to enter the desired text. .

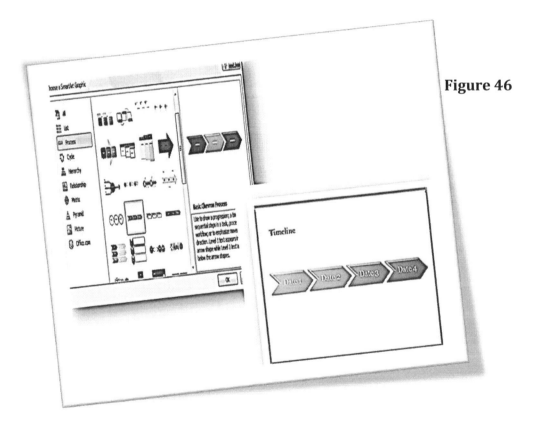

Figure 46

SmartArt Graphic Options

Lists: Select this option to create visual effects for bulleted items.

Process: An option suitable for depicting routes, procedures and progression.

Cycle: Represents a sequence of stages, tasks, or events in a circular flow.

Hierarchy: Shows hierarchical information or reporting relationships

Relationship: Depicts connections, links, or a correlation.

Matrix: Used for concepts, relationships sequenced or grouped blocks of information.

Pyramid: Used to show containment, proportional, or interconnected relationships.

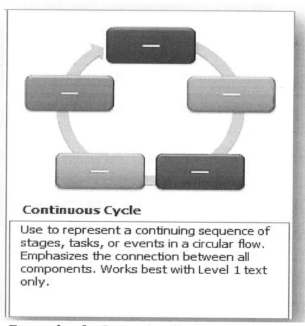

Continuous Cycle

Use to represent a continuing sequence of stages, tasks, or events in a circular flow. Emphasizes the connection between all components. Works best with Level 1 text only.

Example of a SmartArt Continuous Cycle
Graphic taken from the SmartArt Gallery
Descriptions taken from the Microsoft SmartArt Gallery

Working with Shapes

Excel comes with a wonderful array of shapes you can use to enhance a worksheet. Whether you need a rectangle, triangle, circle or star, Excel likely has just what you need. You can find the Shapes button on the Insert tab. See Figure 47 below.

Place a Shape within a Worksheet

1. Click into the cell where you want the shape to appear.

2. Click on the Insert tab.

3. Click on the Shapes dropdown box.

4. Select the desired shape

5. Hold down your left mouse button and then drag your mouse to draw and size the shape.

Figure 47

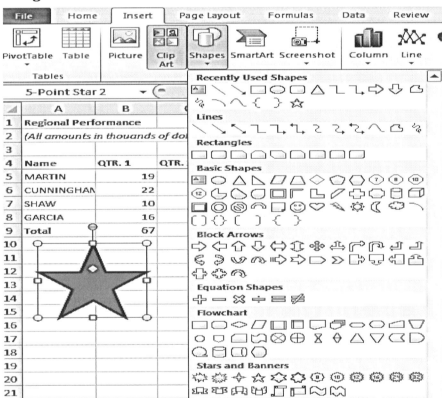

Excel Templates

Microsoft Excel comes bundled with a variety of templates you may find helpful. For example, if you want to create a balance sheet, invoice, or packing slip, you will likely find it in Excel's templates gallery.

To View the Excel Templates Gallery

1. Click on the File tab.
2. Select the New menu option.
3. Choose templates.
4. Select the desired template.
5. Choose the Download button.

Figure 48

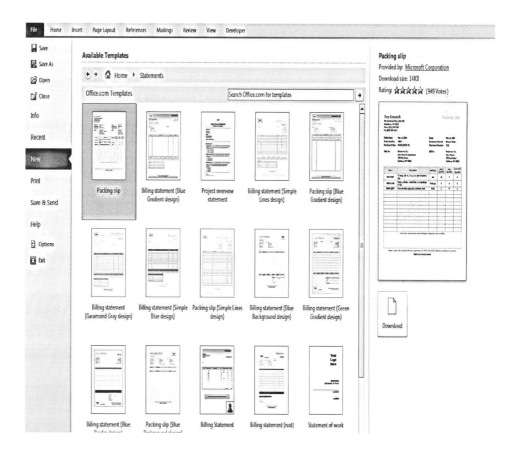

Example of an Excel Receipt Template

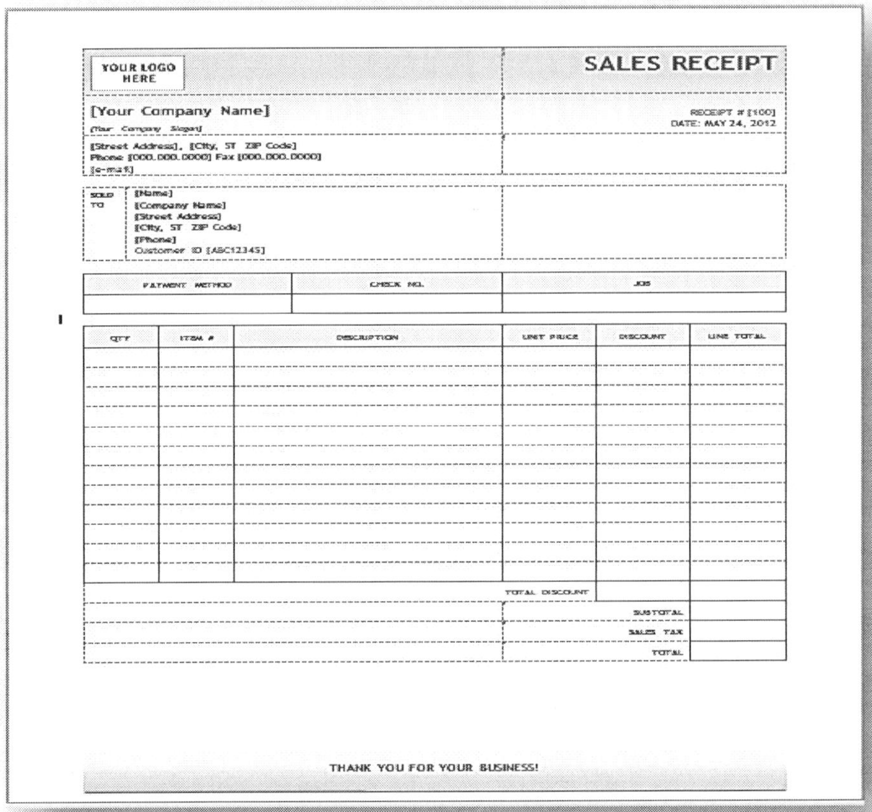

Figure 49

Templates are easy to work with, can be edited and can save you from having to create these types of documents from scratch. To use a template like the one depicted above, just begin typing within the pre-designed fields. Be sure to examine your templates, as several of them are designed with formulas that will calculate items such as totals, interest, tax, etc.

Chapter 10

MS-EXCEL RIBBONS & TABS

- *File Tab*

- *Home Tab*

- *Insert Tab*

- *Page Layout Tab*

- *Formulas Tab*

- *Data Tab*

- *Review Tab*

- *View Tab*

- *Developer Tab*

Microsoft Excel Ribbons & Tabs

The File Tab - Backstage View

Figure 50

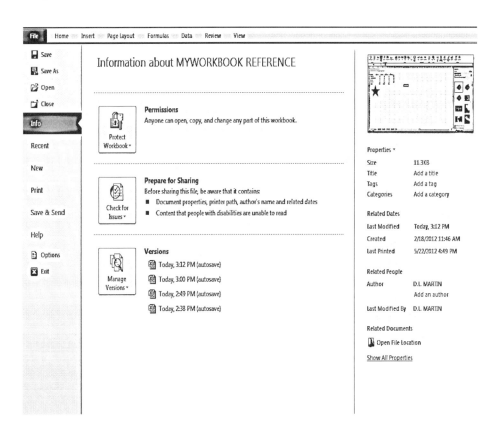

On the File tab, you will find a variety of menu options such as Info, Open, Save As, and Print. You can also exit from Excel by using this menu. In addition, you will find an online Help program if you need more information regarding an Excel feature or function.

When you become a little more proficient with Excel, you may want to select the Options menu to customize the Excel environment. From the File tab's backstage view, you can also see properties for your workbook, such as file size, and author.

Home

On this ribbon are features you will need on a frequent basis. For example here you can change your font, copy and paste, apply number, comma or the currency style to your cells.

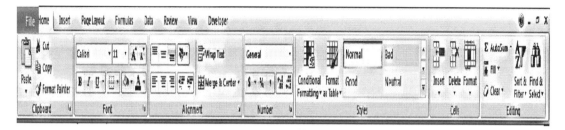

Insert

Use the Insert tab functions to place a chart, Clip Art, headers, and/or footers into your worksheet. Also available are tables, hyperlinks and WordArt.

Page Layout

You will find the Page Layout ribbon to be particularly useful if you want to adjust margins, turn on/off gridlines in your worksheet or insert page breaks. Use this tab to change worksheet orientation or set the print area within a worksheet.

Formulas

On the Formulas tab, you will find Excel's Function Library, auditing tools and calculation features. To see the formulas in your worksheet choose the Show Formulas button.

Data

The Data ribbon contains all the functionality you will need to sort and organize the data in your worksheet. Sort options include ascending and descending order.

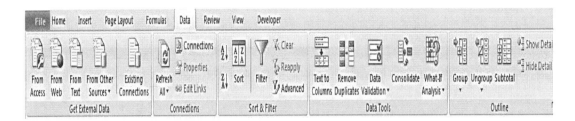

Review

Here is where you will find important features such as Excel's Spelling & Grammar feature. You can also use this tab to access options for protecting your worksheet.

View

The View ribbon contains functions that will permit you control the magnification of your document on the screen. It will also allow you to choose how to arrange multiple windows, turn on/off gridlines, and the Freeze Panes button.

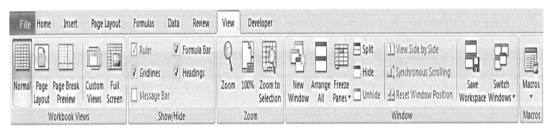

Developer

This ribbon is for the more advanced user who is ready to create macros (programs) to automate tasks in Excel.

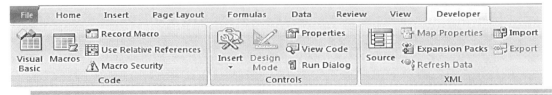

"The audience only pays attention as long as you know where you are going."

Philip Crosby

Chapter 11

GETTING STARTED WITH POWERPOINT

- ***Identify Issues Involved in Presentation Planning***
- ***Launch PowerPoint***
- ***Add New Slides to a Presentation***
- ***Save a Presentation***
- ***Open And Close a PowerPoint Presentation***
- ***View Multiple Presentations Simultaneously***

🕐 ***The Estimated Time to Completed These Tasks is 16 Minutes.***

Before You Begin Working with PowerPoint

Assume you have been tasked with putting together a PowerPoint presentation. There are a several questions to consider before you begin.

❖ What kinds of information will your presentation include?

❖ How many slides will you need to prepare?

❖ Is there any intellectual property or branding issues to consider?

❖ How many people will be speaking?

❖ Will you need handouts, notes pages or an outline?

A Little Planning Goes a Long Way

❖ Prepare a rough draft of your presentation on paper first. This will speed up the design phase when you begin working within the PowerPoint application.

❖ Keep in mind that the best presentations are rehearsed. Be sure to allocate enough time for preparation, and ensure that everyone who will be speaking has seen the presentation, and rehearsed with the PowerPoint application.

❖ During the design phase of the presentation, you may consider, or others may ask you to insert graphics into your slides. Be sure that you are legally permitted to use those graphics. Corporate logos and images of discernible individuals generally require the owner's permission before they may be used. This is especially important if those graphics are being used for commercial purposes.

❖ Have everyone involved in the presentation review it for spelling, typographical or grammatical errors; you will be glad you did, as the appearance of these kinds of mistakes can mar an otherwise flawless presentation.

Launching the Microsoft PowerPoint Application

Launch the Microsoft PowerPoint application from your desktop by clicking the Start Button located in the lower left-hand side of your screen. Look for the icon depicted below.

To open the PowerPoint application, look for this icon.

The Microsoft PowerPoint Environment – *Slide View*

Figure 51

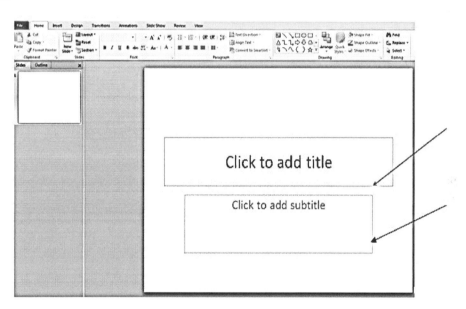

After launching Microsoft PowerPoint, a new blank presentation will open. Every effective presentation begins with a title slide. Fortunately, PowerPoint creates a title slide for you. All you have to do is type the desired text into the placeholders. For example, see Figure 51. Note that a blank slide template appears ready for you to type the title of your presentation. See the three easy steps below.

1. Click into the **add title** placeholder and begin typing.

2. To add a subtitle, just click into the **Click to add subtitle** placeholder.

3. Type your subtitle.

Example of an Inserted Title and Subtitle in Slide View

Figure 52

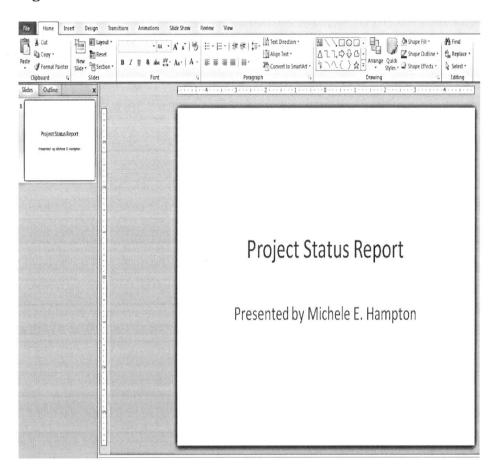

Examine Figure 52 and you will see that the slide view window is actually divided into two parts. PowerPoint displays a thumbnail view of your slides on the left side of the screen.

Now look a little closer at Figure 52 and you will see that just behind the Slides tab there is the Outline view tab. As you create your presentation, PowerPoint prepares an outline of each slide. Click on the Slides tab if you want to keep the thumbnails in view, as you create your presentation.

Click on the [**X**] button adjacent to the Outline tab if you do not want to view the thumbnails or the outline view while you work.

Adding New Slides to a Presentation

Now you are ready to begin adding additional slides to your presentation. Notice that on the ribbon of the Home tab, there is a button nicely marked "**New Slide**".

To Add New Slides

1. Click on the Home tab.
2. Click on the New Slide button.

Presentations typically include just the "power points" you want to discuss. For this reason, you will find the ability to insert bulleted text very useful for depicting key points in your presentation.

To Add Bulleted Text

1. Click your mouse into the bulleted text placeholder
2. Type your text.
3. Press Enter after each line of text.

The icons depicted in the placeholder in Figure 53 represent the types of objects you can place within a PowerPoint presentation. These objects include, tables, charts, clip art, video and SmartArt.

Figure 53

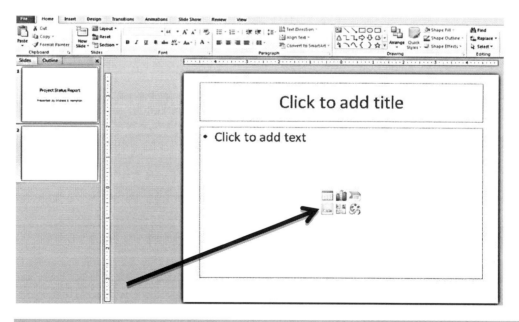

Save a Presentation

After you have created your presentation, you will want to save it. Make it a practice to save your work at regular intervals.

To Save a Presentation

1. Click on the File tab.
2. Click on the Save menu option.
3. Type a name for your presentation.
4. Click on the Save button.
5. Choose OK.

Use the Save As menu option if you are working with a previously saved presentation and need another copy in a different file format. Alternatively, you can use Save As to save an existing file under a different filename. To save a copy of your presentation as a PDF file, you should select the File tab, and then choose the Save As button. Be sure to select the desired file type.

Figure 54

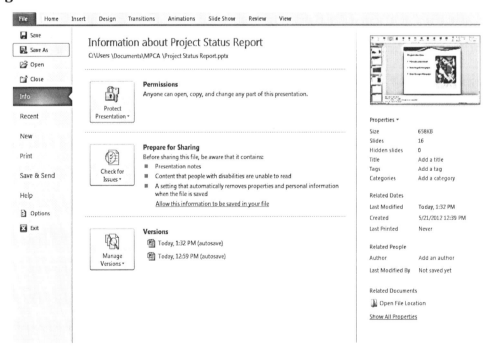

Opening and Closing a PowerPoint Presentation

If you are like me, you prefer to work around as little clutter as possible. When I am done working with a particular presentation, I close it. When you close a presentation, PowerPoint simply stores the presentation, but the application itself remains open. Keep in mind that there is no set limit on the number of presentations you may have open at one time.

To Close a Presentation

1. Click on the File tab.
2. Choose the close icon located near the top of the menu.

To Open an Existing Presentation

Obviously, an existing presentation is one that has previously been saved to your hard drive, flash drive or floppy drive. To open an existing presentation:

1. Click on the File tab.
2. Choose the Open menu option.
3. Locate the desired file.
4. Click on the Open button.

Viewing Multiple Presentations Simultaneously

As mentioned previously, it is possible to open and view more than one presentation at a time. In fact, this can be quite advantageous if you need to compare and/or move data between two different presentations. One of the most helpful features is Arrange All located on the View tab. This button will place your presentations side by side.

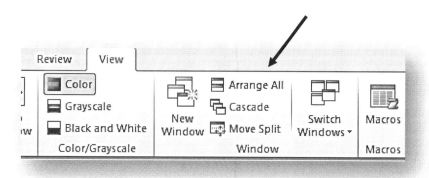

My Notes:

Chapter 12

FORMATTING & PRINTING

- *Change Slide Layout*

- *Apply a Design Theme*

- *Insert a Footer*

- *Insert a Header*

- *List Five Time-Saving Printing Tips*

- *Print a Presentation*

🕐 *The Estimated Time to Complete These Tasks is* <u>*13*</u> *Minutes.*

Changing Slide Layout

As you add new slides to your presentation, you may decide that you would prefer a different layout. PowerPoint comes with more than a dozen different layouts. In less than five seconds, you can change the layout of any given slide by selecting the Layout dropdown box pictured in Figure 55.

To Change the Slide Layout

1. Click on the slide containing the layout you wish to change.

2. Choose the Home tab.

3. Click on the Layout dropdown box.

4. Choose the desired slide layout.

Figure 55

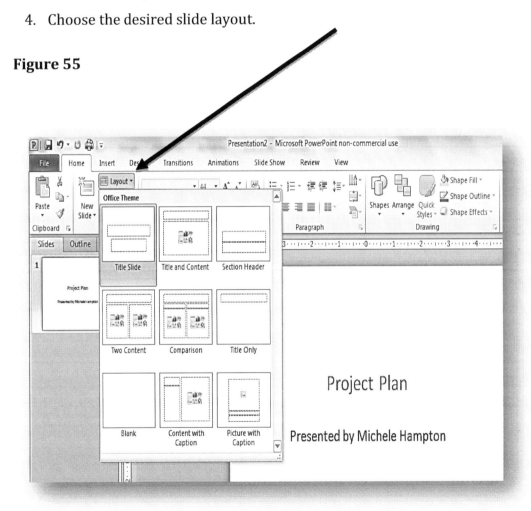

Applying a Design Theme

Maintaining and sustaining the attention of your audience should be a priority in any presentation, and choosing a theme for your presentation will likely be one of your more challenging tasks. There are so many choices, and external factors to consider. For example, if you are preparing a presentation for your employer, you may want to consider the use of colors consistent with your organization's brand. Assuming you have complete flexibility, consider that PowerPoint comes bundled with more than 60 design themes that combine well-matched colors, and fonts. See Figure 56.

To Apply a Design Theme

1. Click on the Design tab.
2. Click on the Themes dropdown box to view the gallery.
3. Select the desired theme.

Figure 56

PowerPoint's Kilter Design Theme

Sample Slide with "Book" Design Applied

Figure 57

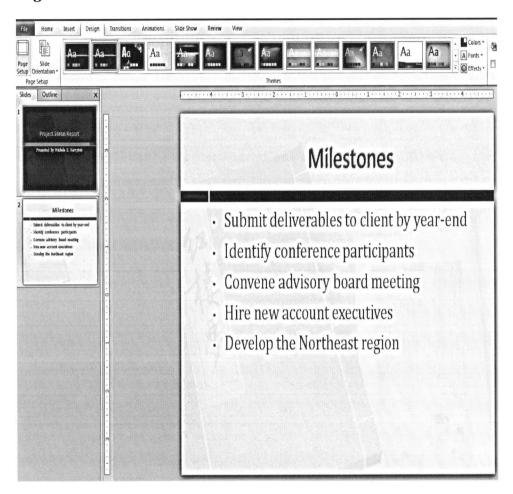

Your presentation can try on various themes. If you hover with your mouse over each of the design themes, PowerPoint will give you a glimpse of what your presentation will look like. See Figure 57. Notice that there are a wide variety of designs.

If you choose a design and decide that, you prefer something different, remember that you can use the Undo button, or simply select another design theme.

Inserting a Footer

Footer is text that appears at the bottom of each of your slides. When you open the Header & Footer dialog box, you can also choose to place the date and/or time, as well as a slide number into your footer. See Figure 58 below.

To Insert a Footer

1. Click on the Insert tab.

2. Click on the Header & Footer button.

3. Select the Slides tab.

4. Click into the Footer check box.

5. Type the text you wish to appear on each slide.

6. Click the Apply to All button.

Figure 58

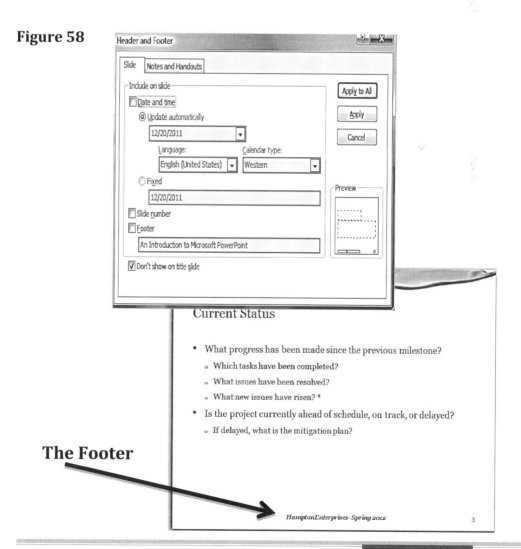

The Footer

Slide with Footer and Slide Number Inserted

Figure 59

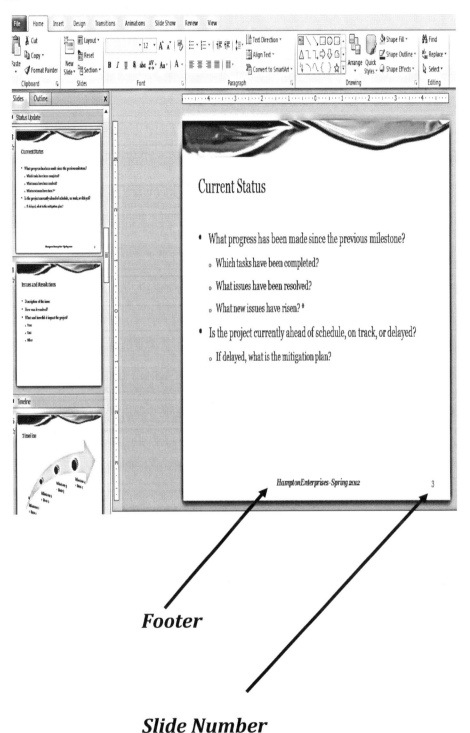

Footer

Slide Number

Inserting a Header

A header is text that is repeated at the top of each PowerPoint slide, notes page and/or handout.   You can also choose to include the date and time. See Figure 60 below.

Figure 60

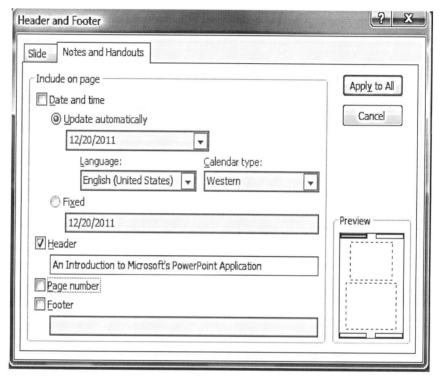

Inserting Headers in Notes Pages and Handouts

1. Click on the Insert tab.

2. Click on the Header & Footer button – located in the Text group.

3. Click the Notes and Handouts tab.

4. Select the Header check box.

5. Type the desired text.

Printing Tips

Check out these PowerPoint printing tips to help you save time and money.

1. Print drafts in pure black and white on your laser printer- color can be expensive.

2. Avoid sending "final" copies to your printer until the presentation has been approved and/or finalized.

3. Print drafts of your presentation in outline or handouts view.

4. Consider whether it is necessary to produce handouts at all. You can for example, provide audience members with an e-mail address, and encourage them to request copies of the presentation if needed. This may actually save a tree or two.

5. Print out an outline of the presentation for the speaker and/or the person who will be running the slide show

Printing a Presentation

Printing Slides

1. Click on the File tab.

2. Select the Print menu option.

3. Click on the Settings button to select slides, handouts or notes pages.

4. Click on the Print button.

Figure 61

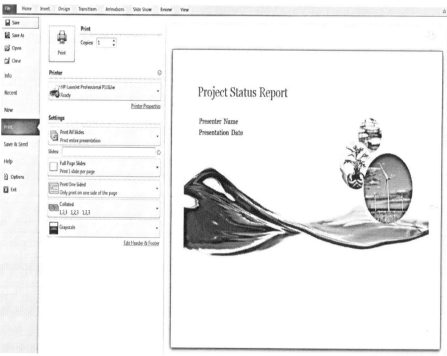

Printing Options:

- **Frame slides**:   Places a border around your Handouts.

- **Scale to fit paper**:   Adjusts the size of your presentation.

- **Handouts:**   Controls how many slides are printed per page.

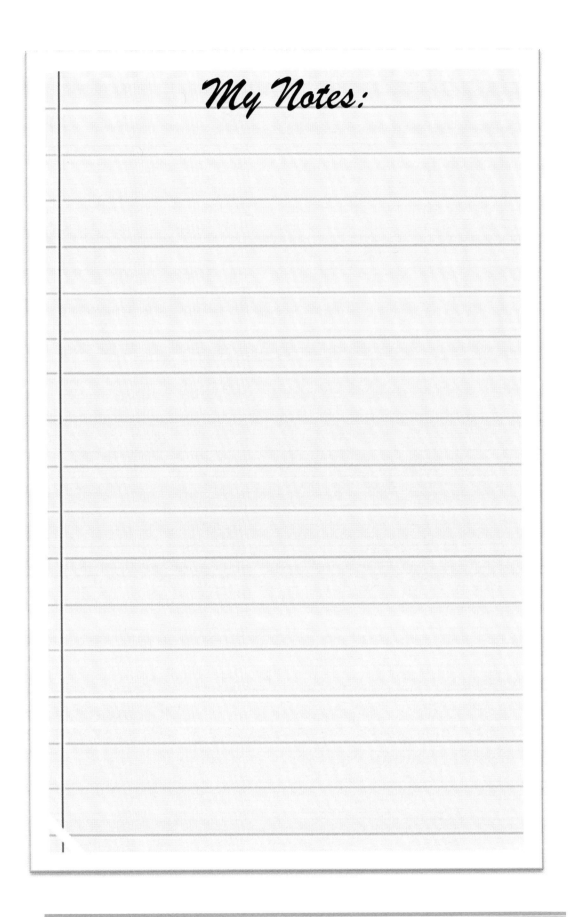

My Notes:

Chapter 13

ENHANCING & MANAGING TEXT

- *Apply Character Formatting*
- *Clear Formatting*
- *Undo Your Last Command*
- *Use the Format Painter*
- *Apply a New Font*
- *Edit with Cut, Copy and Paste*
- *Use the Spelling & Grammar Feature*

🕑 *The Estimated Time to Complete These Tasks is 15 Minutes.*

Applying Character Formatting

You can focus your reader's attention by applying Microsoft PowerPoint's text formatting features. With one keystroke and in less than five seconds, you can bold, underline, italicize, color or change the typeface.

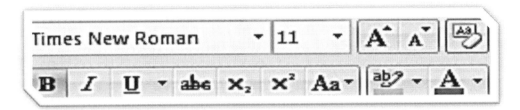

Apply Bold Text

Drag your mouse to select the desired text, and then click on the **Bold** button. Repeat this process to underline (**U**) or italicize (**I**) text.

Clear Formatting

If you change your mind, simply select the desired text, and then click on the Clear Formatting button located on the Home tab. This will erase any formatting such as bold or underline from the selected text.

Undo Your Last Command

Note, that you can also undo your last keystrokes by clicking the Undo button. You will find this button located on the Quick Access Toolbar.

Save Time with Format Painter

If you have worked with Microsoft Word, then you already know what a time-saver the Format Painter can be. This feature allows you to copy the character formatting of a word and then apply it to another word, sentence or paragraph.

1. Select the word that contains the desired formatting.

2. Click on the Format Painter to copy the formatting.

3. Select the destination text to apply the desired formatting.

Apply a New Font

PowerPoint comes with more than 75 different fonts, and it is very easy to change these fonts on the fly. In addition, there is also a wide selection of serif and san serif fonts. Serif fonts have little edges or "feet" on each letter. Sans Serifs (sans meaning without) lack these feet. **Arial** is an example of a sans serif font, while **Georgia** is an example of a serif font. In addition to changing the typeface, you will also want to become familiar with the Font Size dropdown box. Notice that fonts are listed in alphabetical order, and appear when you click on the Font dropdown box. See Figure 62. Notice that just to the right is the Font Size box.

To Change a Font

1. Click on the Home tab.
2. Select the text to be changed.
3. Click on the Font dropdown box and choose the desired font.
4. Click on the Size button if you also wish to change the size of the text as well.

Figure 62

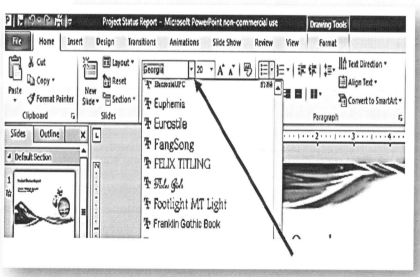

It is generally easier to read serif fonts. However, what you ultimately select will depend on your taste and individual needs. You may also want to check with your employer to find out if a specific font has been chosen for all office correspondence.

Working with Cut, Copy, and Paste

Often you will want to copy text. Alternatively, you can permanently move text to another part of your document. PowerPoint's Cut, Copy and Paste feature allows you to do this in mere seconds. The copied text is moved to the Clipboard. Think of the Clipboard as a magical place where data waits for you to decide where to place it. There are at least three different ways to copy and/or move text in PowerPoint. For example, if you want to copy text, follow the four easy steps below.

1. Select the text you want to copy.

2. Click on the Copy button.

3. Place your mouse where you want the copied text to appear.

4. Right click your mouse button and then choose Paste.

Alternatively, you can highlight the selected text, and then use the short-cut keystroke, Ctrl + C to copy. Use Ctrl + V to paste.

To Delete or Cut Text

1. Select the text you want to cut.

2. Click on the Cut (scissors icon) located in the Clipboard group

You can also select the text you want to delete and then press the delete key.

Spelling & Grammar

Microsoft PowerPoint contains a spell check feature that will automatically check your document for common spelling and grammatical errors. In addition, you can quickly spell check a word by selecting it, and then clicking on the Spelling & Grammar button. Be advised that proper nouns and words typed in all capitals are generally **not** reviewed by the Spelling feature.

1. Click on the Review tab, and then click on the Spelling & Grammar button.

2. To accept a suggested correction, click the Accept button.

Note, that PowerPoint also contains a handy thesaurus. To use the thesaurus, simply select the desired word, and then right click your mouse button; choose the suggested synonym or choose Thesaurus.

Be Sure To Review Your Work!

An effective presentation should capture and sustain the audience's attention. Thus, it is important to both carefully select your "power points" and check to ensure your presentation is error free. You will want to begin by using the application's built-in spelling and grammar checking feature before you print out your first draft, and again after your final edits. Be advised that it is always best to have others check your presentation for errors as well. It is often difficult for us to be objective about our work. Thus, despite your best intentions, you will not likely catch all of your own mistakes.

Keep in mind that PowerPoint has its limits. As has been discussed, PowerPoint will generally not flag as misspelled proper nouns or acronyms. Check, check and then check again. If your presentation is projected onto a large screen with fonts larger than 24 points, any errors will stand out like a red flag.

****

My Notes:

Chapter 14

TEMPLATES, TABLES & IMAGES

- ***Work with PowerPoint Templates***

- ***Create a Table***

- ***Enhance a Table with Styles***

- ***Insert Clip Art, Pictures or Other Media***

- ***Adjust the Size of a Picture or Illustration***

- ***Insert a Microsoft Excel Chart***

- ***Use SmartArt to Enhance a Presentation***

- ***Create Shapes***

- ***Enhance a Slide Show with Animations and Transitions***

🕐 *The Estimated Time to Complete These Tasks is __30__ Minutes.*

Working with Templates

What you will likely appreciate about PowerPoint templates is that they can give you a bit of a kick-start when you are not sure how to begin the design process. Moreover, templates can offer ideas for your own presentation in terms of layout, color and design. You will find a variety of templates when you choose New from the File tab. See Figure 63. Additionally, if you are looking for a particular type of template, i.e. status report, simply type the words status report into the Search Office.com for templates field.

.

1. Click on the File tab.

2. Choose the New menu option.

3. Click on the Sample templates icon to view the built-in templates.

4. Click on the desired template.

5. Click on the Create button.

Figure 63

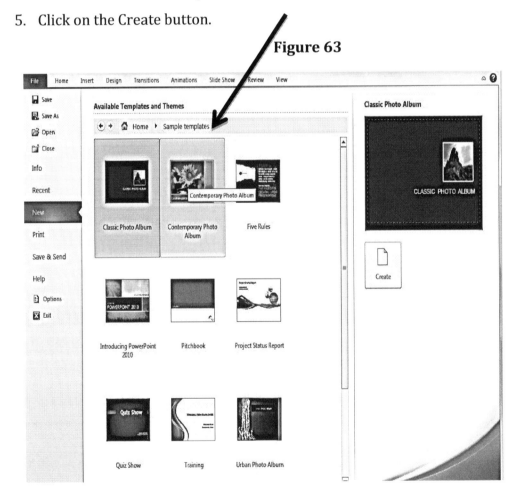

Creating a Table

A table can be used to organize data, make it easier to type, and edit text. In less than five minutes, you can move seamlessly through the table and enhance it for a very polished and professional look.

1. Click on the Home tab.
2. Choose the New Slide button.
3. Select the Insert Table icon (located in the large placeholder).
4. Choose the Insert Table button.
5. Choose the number of columns and rows, and then choose OK.

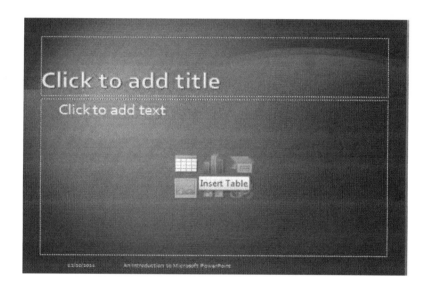

Setting a Pretty Table

You can enhance your table by using the Table Styles feature. When you click anywhere within your table, the Design tab appears. Simply click on the Design tab, and then choose the desired table design from the Table Styles Gallery.

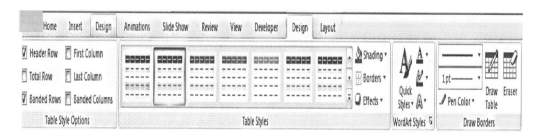

Slide with Inserted Finished Table and Short Menu

Figure 64

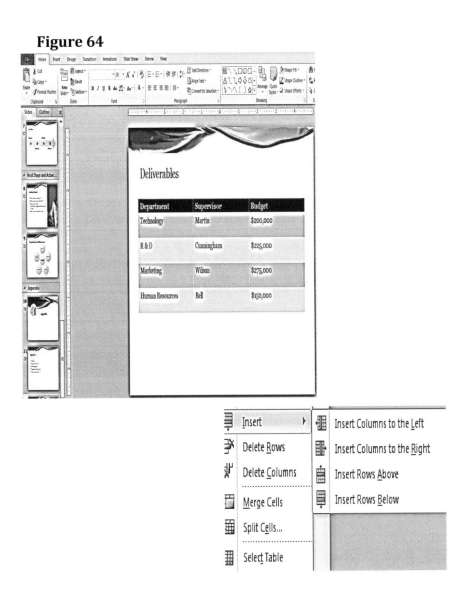

To quickly add rows and columns to your table, merely double-click anywhere in the table to activate the Table Tools tab. Select a row or column within the table and then right-click your mouse button to access the short menu.

You can choose to insert rows and columns or delete selected rows and columns. See Figure 64 above. In addition, you can also choose to merge or split any selected cells.

Clip Art, Illustrations and Other Media

Pictures really do help tell your story, and fortunately, PowerPoint makes the placement of various media types within a document very easy to do. The Clip Art a gallery contains illustrations, videos, photographs and audio files that come bundled with PowerPoint.

In general, personal photographs are stored in your My Pictures folder. Therefore, if you want to insert the photograph you took of your dog Fido, choose the Picture button located on the Insert tab. On the other hand, if you are looking for some illustrations to spice up your PTA flyer you may want to open the Clip Art Gallery. Place your cursor in your document where you want the picture, photograph, video or audio file to appear, and then do the following:

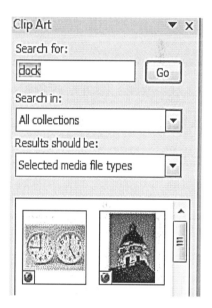

1. Click on the Insert tab.

2. Select the Clip Art or Picture button.

3. Type the name of the object you want to find.

4. Click on the Go button.

5. Click on the desired image.

Adjusting the Size of Photographs or Clip Art

After you select your photograph or clip art, PowerPoint places it into your presentation surrounded by handles. See the clock image below.

To make the image larger or smaller, simply hover with your mouse over any of the handles, and notice the double arrow. When the double arrow appears, hold down your left mouse button and drag it left or right to size the image.

Slide with Clip Art Inserted

Figure 65

As mentioned previously, the Clip Art Gallery comes bundled with a variety of illustrations, photographs, videos and audios. For purposes of searching the Gallery, you can control the type of objects the Clip Art Gallery retrieves.

 If you click on the Results should be field, you may choose to limit or expand your search for various media types, such as photographs, videos, illustrations and audio files by clicking into desired media checkbox. See Figure 65 above.

Inserting a Microsoft Excel Chart

Presentations that include numerical data may be hard to understand and somewhat difficult to communicate. To help the audience interpret numerical data, consider the use of a Microsoft Excel chart. PowerPoint's Title and Content Slide includes an easy-to-use chart design feature. After you select this feature, an Excel datasheet will appear, allowing you to customize and edit your data as needed. See Figure 66.

1. Select the Home tab.

2. Click on the New Slide button.

3. Select the Chart button (*within the Title and Content placeholder*).

4. Enter the data for your chart.

5. Save and close the worksheet.

Figure 66

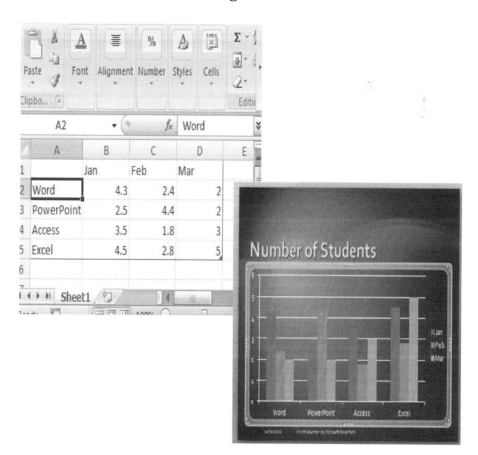

The Insert Chart Button

Notice how the range is highlighted in the Excel worksheet in Figure 67. PowerPoint provides mock data as a guide; simply type your data into the selected range.

Figure 67

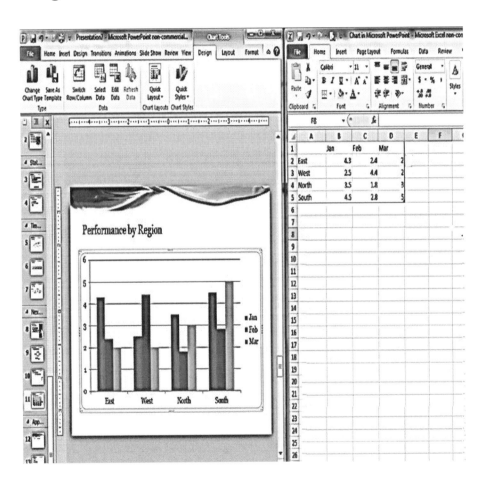

Any time you want to edit your chart, simply point to it and double-click your left mouse button. This will activate the Chart Tools tab, and open your worksheet.

When the datasheet is activated, PowerPoint will display a Microsoft Excel ribbon containing chart buttons and features to facilitate editing.

Work with SmartArt

To create a visually appealing presentation, consider the use of Microsoft's SmartArt. The SmartArt gallery comes with more than 40 objects including organizational charts, flow charts and process symbols. For practice, try creating the organizational chart depicted in Figure 68.

To Create an Organizational Chart

1. Select the Insert tab.

2. Place your cursor where you want the chart to appear.

3. Click on the SmartArt button.

4. Click on Hierarchy within the Navigation pane.

5. Choose the desired layout.

6. Click into the placeholders and enter the names and titles of the individuals.

Figure 68

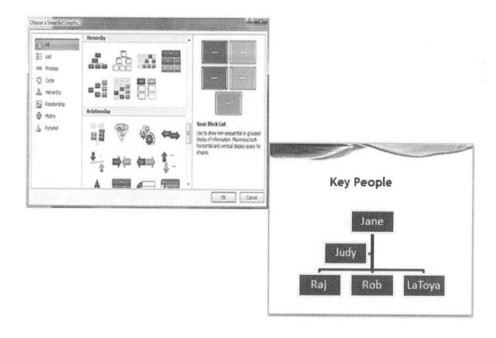

SmartArt Graphic Options

- **Lists:**   Select this option to create visual effects for bulleted items.

- **Process:**   An option suitable for depicting routes, procedures and progression.

- **Cycle:**   Represents a sequence of stages, tasks, or events in a circular flow.

- **Hierarchy:**   Shows hierarchical information or reporting relationships.

- **Relationship:** Depicts connections, links, or a correlation

- **Matrix:**   Used for concepts, relationships, or grouped blocks of information.

- **Pyramid:**   Shows containment, proportional, or interconnected relationships.

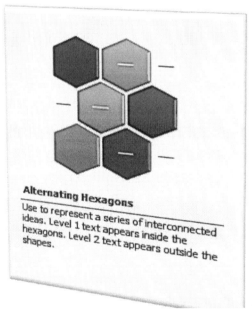

Alternating Hexagons

Use to represent a series of interconnected ideas. Level 1 text appears inside the hexagons. Level 2 text appears outside the shapes.

Example of a SmartArt Alternating Hexagons
Descriptions taken from the SmartArt Gallery

Working with Shapes

PowerPoint comes with a wonderful array of shapes you can use to enhance your slides. Whether you need a rectangle, triangle, circle or star, PowerPoint likely has just what you need. You can find PowerPoint's Shapes within the Illustrations group, located on the Insert Ribbon. See Figure 69.

To Insert a Shape

1. Click into the slide where you want the shape to appear.

2. Click on the Insert tab.

3. Click on the Shapes dropdown box.

4. Select the desired shape.

5. Hold down your left mouse button and then drag your mouse to draw and size the shape.

Figure 69

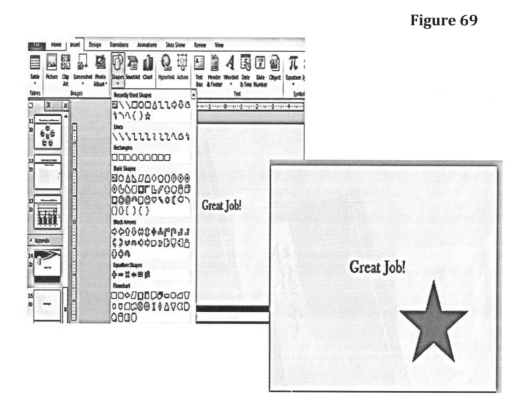

Enhancing a Slide Show with Animations

Microsoft's PowerPoint application can assist you with sustaining your viewer's interest throughout your presentation. The application contains a variety of animation options you can incorporate in one or several different slides.

To explore the available animation options, select the Animations tab and then click on the drop down box in the Animation group to view them. PowerPoint will display the animation effect for you.

1. Select the Animations tab.

2. Scroll to view the Animation options.

3. Click on the desired animation.

Figure 70

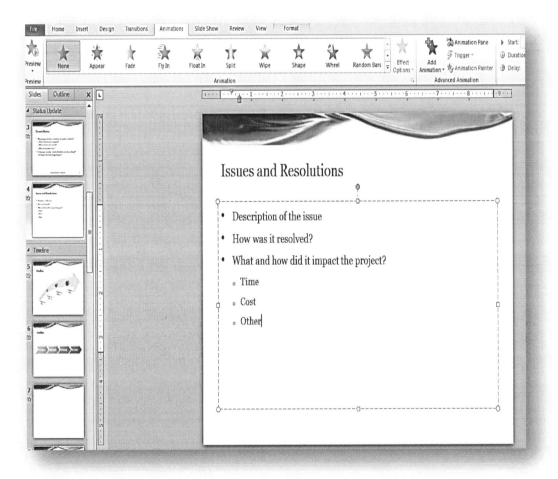

Add Slide Show Transitions

If you want to create transitions between slides, consider the use of PowerPoint's transitions feature. You will be happy to know that you can apply transitions to slides just as you applied animation effects. For an example, see the Honeycomb transition depicted in Figure 71. PowerPoint makes more than 30 transitions available to you. In addition, you can try on each transition. Simply click on the desired transition and PowerPoint will instantly display the effect on the screen.

Be judicious in your use of both animations and transitions. You risk obscuring your message, if you incorporate too many special effects into your presentation.

To Apply a Transition

1. Select the desired slide.
2. Select the Transitions tab.
3. Click on the desired transition.

Figure 71

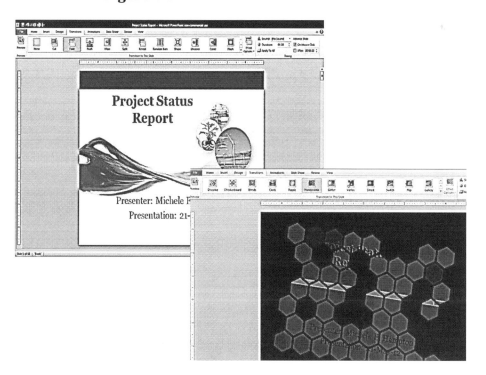

My Notes:

Chapter 15

VIEWING & RUNNING

A

SLIDE SHOW

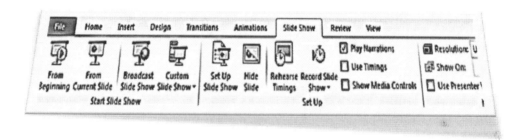

- **Work With Slide View Buttons**

- **Rearrange Slides**

- **Use the Set Up Slide Show Buttons**

- **Rehearse Timings**

- **Run a Presentation in Slide Show View**

🕐 *The Estimated Time to Complete These Tasks is 10-15 Minutes.*

Working in Slide View

If you examine the lower right side of the PowerPoint window, you will notice several tiny buttons pictured above and enlarged in Figure 73. These buttons allow you to display your presentation in four views: Normal, Slide Sorter, Reading View and Slide Show. The default view, or view you will see each time you open PowerPoint is slide view depicted in Figure 72.

You can also adjust the magnification of your slides on screen by clicking on the Zoom button. Alternatively, you can click on the plus or minus sign to increase or decrease the magnification. See the close-up in Figure 73.

Figure 72

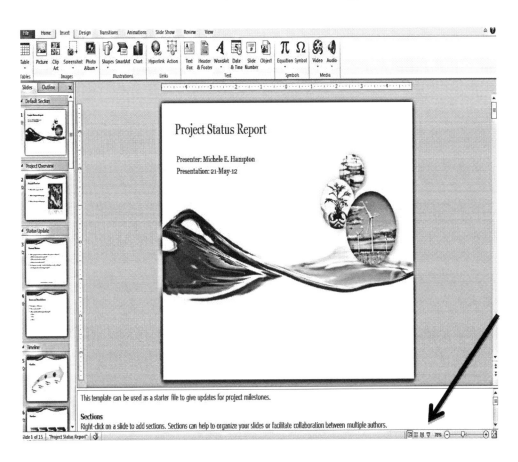

Figure 73

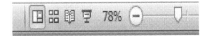

Rearranging Slides with Slide Sorter View

There is no doubt that you will inevitably have a need to change the order of your slides. For this reason, you will really come to appreciate PowerPoint's Slide Sorter. When you choose the Slide Sorter view, PowerPoint will number and display all of your slides side-by-side. See Figure 74. You can easily change the order of any slide's appearance in your presentation.

To Rearrange Slides

1. Click on the slide you want to move, (*A black guide line will appear.*)

2. Hold down your left mouse button, drag, and then drop the slide into the desired location.

Figure 74

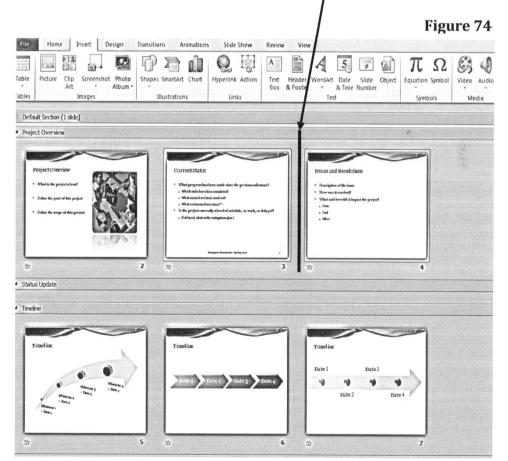

Using the Set Up Slide Show Feature

With PowerPoint, you can determine which slides to display, whether to advance your slides manually or set up your presentation to run continuously. You can also mark your slides during your presentation. In addition, you can also choose a pen color. To do this, you will need to select the Slide Show tab, and then choose Set Up Slide Show. This button is located within the Set Up group, located on the Slide Show tab. See Figure 75.

 If you have a slide in your presentation that you wish to retain, but not display for the audience, select the desired slide, and then choose the Hide Slide button.

Rehearse Timings

 Use the Rehearse Timings button to record the length of your presentation. This feature will launch the slide show view and a timer so you can determine how long each slide should be displayed on the screen.

Figure 75

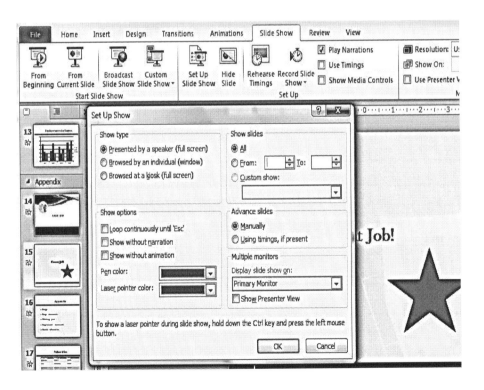

Slide Show View

To see how your final on-screen presentation will look, click on the Slide Show button at the bottom right hand side of the PowerPoint window. You will not see the application's ribbons and tabs. Once you are in slide show view. You can access the short menu and advance through your slide show by clicking the right-mouse button. See the enlarged menu depicted in Figure 76.

When you access the short menu, you can advance your slides by pressing your right mouse button, and then choosing the Next menu option. Other options include Previous, and Go to, which is handy if you want to go to a specific slide.

Black Screen: Makes an all-black screen appear.

White Screen: Makes an all-white screen appear.

Pointer Options: A free-hand drawing tool enabling you to mark slides as you present them.

Highlighter: Allows you to highlight text or graphics in slide show mode.

Figure 76

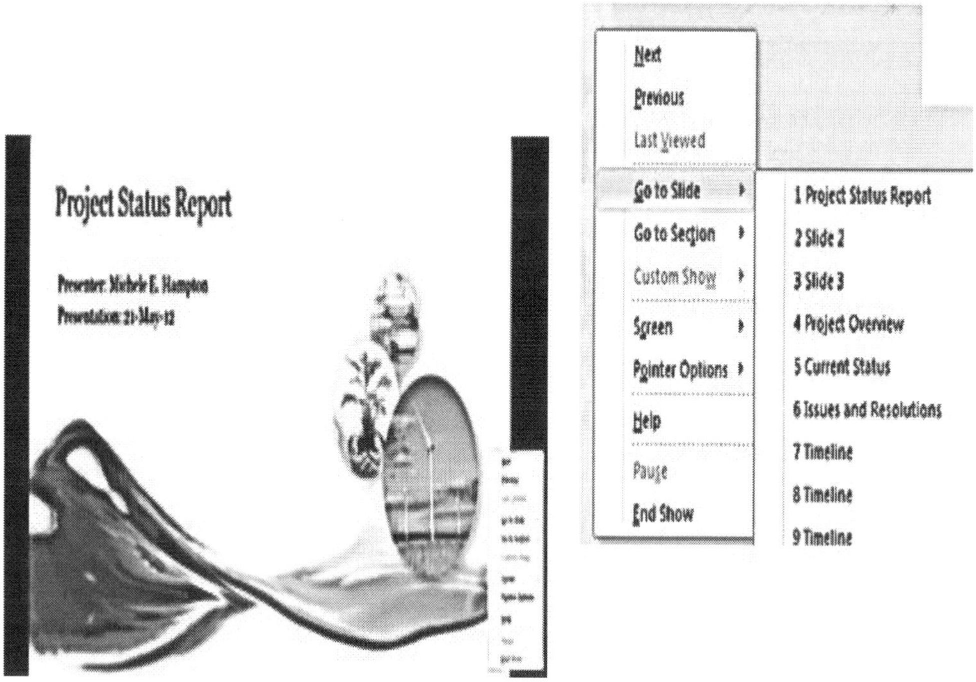

My Notes:

Chapter 16

PowerPoint Ribbons & Tabs

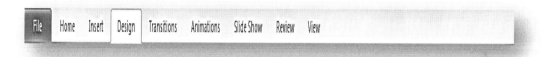

- *File Tab*
- *Home Tab*
- *Insert Tab*
- *Design Tab*
- *Animations Tab*
- *Transitions Tab*
- *Slide Show Tab*
- *Review Tab*
- *View Tab*
- *Format Tab*

The File Tab and Backstage View

On the File tab, you will find a variety of menu options such as Info, Open, Save As, and Print. You can also exit from PowerPoint by using this menu. In addition, you will find an online Help program if you need more information regarding a PowerPoint feature or function.

Figure 77

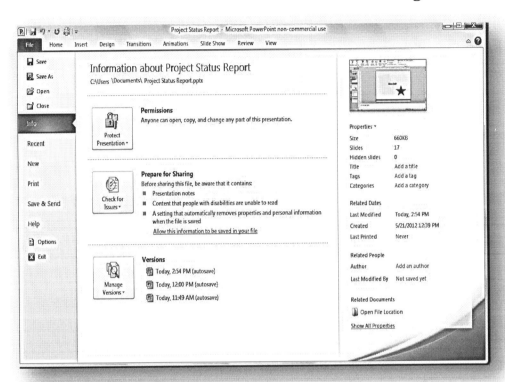

When you become a little more experienced, you may want to select the Options menu to customize the PowerPoint environment.
See Figure 77.

From the backstage view, you can also see properties for your presentation, such as file size, number of slides and author.

Note: On the following pages, you will find screen shots of ribbons and tabs from the Microsoft PowerPoint 2010 application. These images are for representational purposes only, and may not depict all of the buttons in your version of the software you may be using.

Home

The Home tab displays a ribbon containing a host of basic slide and text formatting options. You can also insert new slides, shapes and slide layouts from this tab.

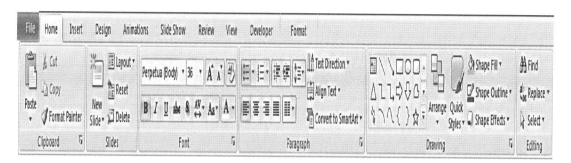

Insert

 Click on the Insert tab to access features like Clip Art, Cover Page, WordArt, headers, footers and SmartArt to name a few. From this tab you can, place photographs, movies, music or Microsoft Excel charts into your presentation.

Design

From this tab, you can apply colorful themes to your presentation, or customize your slides at any time. You can also change slide orientation, colors and fonts.

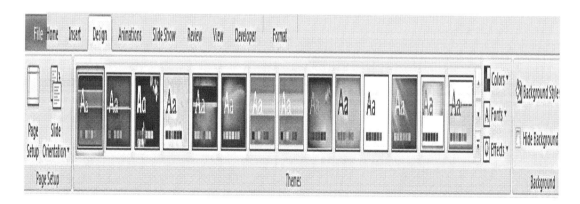

Animations

To sustain the interest of your audience throughout your presentation try adding animations to your slides. This works best with bulleted text. From this tab, you can also see a preview of your animations.

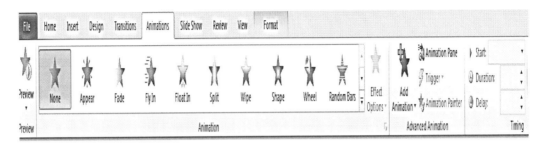

Transitions

You can create a transition from one slide to another using PowerPoint's Transition feature. Select the slide you wish to apply the transition to, and then, select the Transition tab. Here you will also find a number of special effects. Select the Preview button to see how the actual effect will appear on screen.

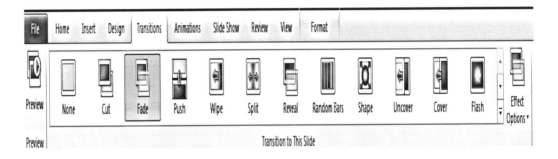

Slide Show

With the options available on this ribbon, you can view and time your presentation (always recommended). You can also choose whether to hide slides. In addition, the Record Narration button will enable you to add a voice track to your presentation.

Review

Before you transmit that document, be sure you select the Review tab. Here you will find great features such as Spelling & Grammar, Thesaurus, and Word Count. You can also add comments to your documents that others can read and respond to through the New and Edit Comment buttons.

View

Use this ribbon to view your slides in various formats, such as slide show, handouts or notes pages. You can also choose to change the magnification of the presentation window. Additionally, you can change the colors of your on-screen presentation with the buttons located within the Color/Grayscale group.

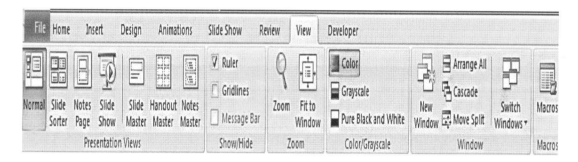

Format

Add artistic effects to shapes, text and graphics using the features available on the Format menu. Be sure to select the text you wish to change and then click on the desired effect.

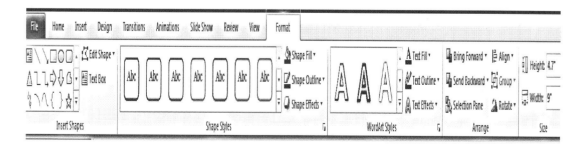

My Notes:

"Organizing is what you do before you do something, so that when you do it, it is not all mixed up."

A. A. Milne

Chapter 17

GETTING STARTED WITH ONENOTE

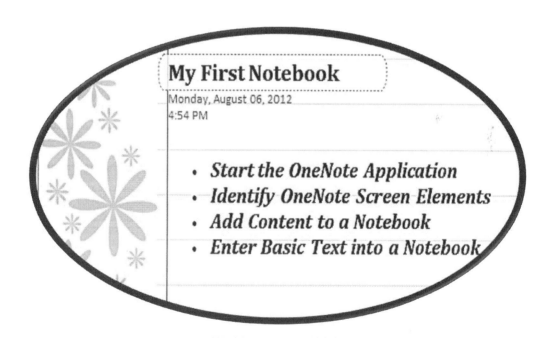

⏱ The Estimated Time to Complete These Tasks is 7 Minutes.

Getting Started with OneNote

 If you are a current Microsoft Office user, you will find the OneNote computing environment very familiar. The ribbons and tabs you have come to know in Microsoft Word, Excel and PowerPoint are also available in OneNote.

You will also find familiar tools such as Format Painter, Spelling, Tables and Shapes. Distinctive new features also await you, such as Research, Linked Notes, Side Notes and Drawing Tools.

Launch the OneNote Application

The first thing we will need to do is to launch the OneNote application by locating its icon. To do this, you will want to follow the steps below.

1. Click on the Start button.
2. Locate the Microsoft OneNote icon and double-click your left mouse button.
3. Choose the New menu option.
4. Select My Computer.
5. Click into the Name field and type a name for your notebook.
6. Click on the Create Notebook button.

Figure 78

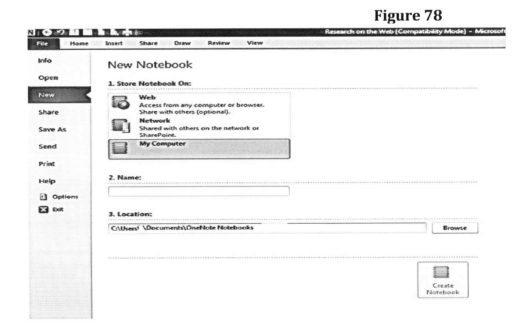

The OneNote Environment

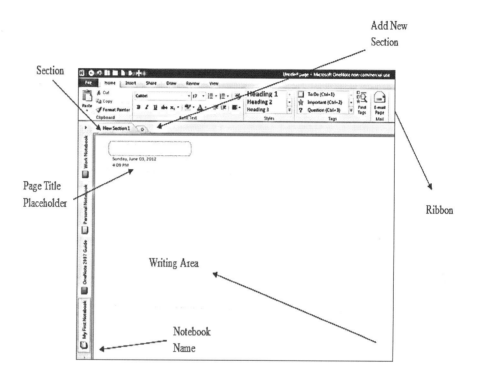

Ribbons, and Tabs, and Groups Oh My!

When OneNote opens beneath the title bar, you will see seven tabs with an activated Home ribbon. Each ribbon is divided into groups. See the illustration above, and examine the groups that appear on Home ribbon, such as Clipboard, Basic Text, Styles, and Tags.

Section/Dividers

OneNote makes it possible to create sections within your notebook. OneNote sections are designed to help you organize your data. Whether you want to organize recipes, homework assignments or your CD collection, you will find the ability to create individual sections within your notebook invaluable. OneNote allows you to add as many additional sections as you need too. Just below the ribbon is the section area. When you open a brand new notebook, one section tab appears along with an Add New Section button. A little later, you will learn how to add pages and sections to your first notebook.

Adding Content to a Notebook

One of the first things you will want to do is to enter a title for the first page of your new notebook. See Figure 79.

Try typing a title within the Page Title Placeholder. After you type your title, notice that the title bar changes. Your notebook is automatically saved under the title you entered.

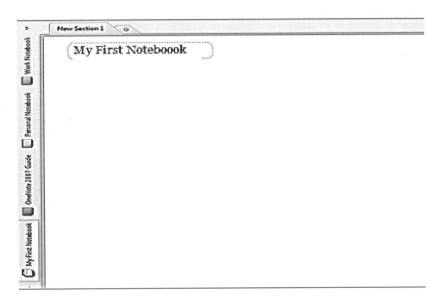

Figure 79

Entering Basic Text

If you click your mouse anywhere within the notebook area, a text window will open, and you will see your cursor flashing. Now you can begin entering basic text into your notebook.

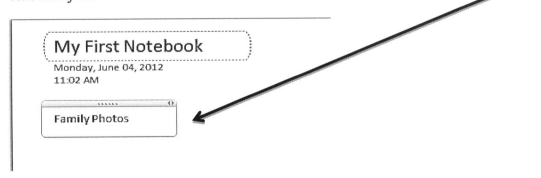

Figure 80

Make Pretty Pages

OneNote Page with Rule Lines and *"Fireworks"* Page Template

Figure 81

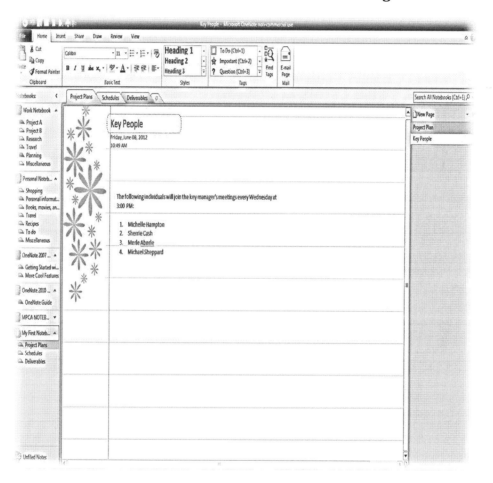

If you are interested adding an artistic element to your notebook, check out the wide variety of page templates that come bundled with Microsoft OneNote. We will share more about page templates in Chapter 18.

My Notes:

Chapter 18

ORGANIZING YOUR NOTEBOOK

- *Add Pages*
- *Use Page Templates*
- *Change Page Colors*
- *Add Rule Lines*
- *Create Sections*
- *Rename a Section*
- *Change Section tab Colors*
- *Rearrange Sections*
- *Insert Space*

🕐 *The Estimated Time to Complete These Tasks is 12 Minutes.*

Adding Pages to a Notebook

In about five seconds, you can add additional pages to your OneNote notebook just as you would add pages to a loose-leaf binder. To add a new page to your notebook

1. Click on the New Page button.
2. Type a title for your new page.

Figure 82

Page Templates

You can spice-up your notebook with a page template. When you click on the New Page drop down box (See Figure 82), several templates will appear on the menu. What is nice about this feature is that the template details will appear when the page is printed.

1. Click on the New Page dropdown box.
2. Choose the desired page design.

Figure 83

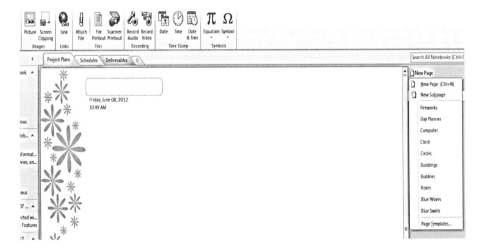

Change the Color of a Notebook Page

Add color to the pages of your notebook by selecting the View Tag. There you will find the Page Color button located within the Page Setup group. When you click on this button, OneNote will display a 16 pastel color pallet. See Figure 84 below. Note that page colors will appear only on screen but will not print to a color-printer.

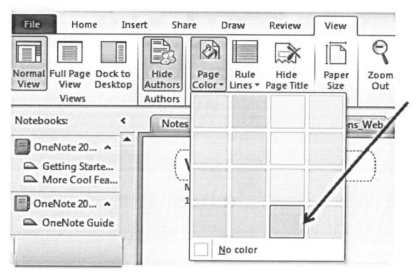

Figure 84

Add Rule lines to a Notebook Page

If you want to recreate the whole notebook look and feel, then you will appreciate OneNote's Rule Lines feature. You can choose from a variety of line styles by clicking on the Rule Lines dropdown box.

Figure 85

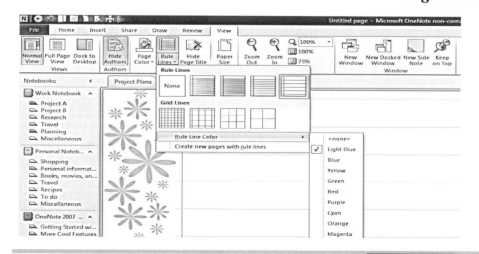

Creating Sections

Figure 86

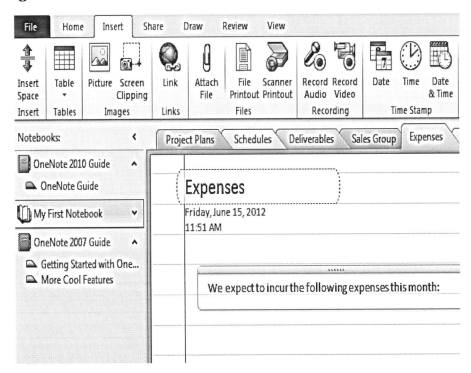

Creating sections within your notebook will help you organize your information. See Figure 86 above and observe that four sections have been created, Project Plans, Schedules, Deliverables and Expenses.

As you will see on the following pages, OneNote makes the addition of sections very quick and easy to do. In seconds, you can create as many sections as you might need for your notebook. In addition, you can color your section tabs, rename sections and rearrange sections within your notebook.

More About Sections

Sections allow you to organize your notebook, and has been mentioned you can create them very quickly. Before you do however, look at the OneNote window in Figure 87 and examine Section 1. OneNote automatically opens with one section each time a new notebook is created. Adjacent to the Section 1 tab is the New Section button. Clicking on this tab will place a new section within your notebook.

Figure 87

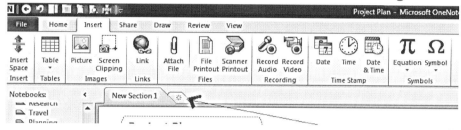

Rename a Section

1. Point to the section tab you want to rename, click your right mouse button.

2. Choose Rename.

3. Type the new section name.

4. Press the enter key.

Change Section Tab Colors   *Figure 88*

1. Point to the section you want to recolor and right click your mouse button.

2. Choose the Section Color option.

3. Choose the desired section color, and then press the enter key.

Rearrange Sections

With OneNote, you have the ability to rearrange your notebook pages and sections. See Figure 89. Assume that you want the Deliverables tab to become the second tab in our notebook too.

1. Point and click on the section you wish to move.

2. Keep your finger on your left mouse button and drag your mouse to the desired location. (You will see what looks like a tiny square or document.) This is the section.

3. With your finger on your left mouse button, drag your mouse to drop the new section into the desired location.

Figure 89

The Insert Space Feature

If you find yourself running out of space, you will adore OneNote's Insert Space feature. In less than sixty-seconds, you can increase the writing area within in your notebook.

Add More Space

1. Click on the Insert tab.

2. Click on the Insert Space button.

3. Move your mouse to the area where you want to insert more space. (A guide will appear.)

4. Click your left mouse button.

CHAPTER 19

FORMATTING & PRINTING

- *Apply Character Formatting*
- *Clear Formatting*
- *Undo the Last Command*
- *Cut, Copy and Paste Text*
- *Use Format Painter*
- *Change Fonts*
- *Apply Styles*
- *Use the Spelling Feature*
- *Print Notebook Pages*

🕐 *The Estimated Time to Complete These Tasks is 20 Minutes.*

Character Formatting

You can focus your reader's attention by applying character formatting. With one keystroke and in less than five seconds, you can apply **bold**, <u>underline</u>, *italics*, or **color**. You can change the typeface of selected text just as you can in Microsoft Word. You will find these tools residing within the Basic Text group, which is located on the Home tab.

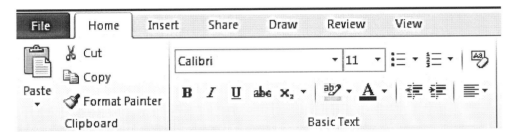

Figure 90

To Apply Bold Text

Select the desired word, and then click on the [B] **Bold** button. Apply underline and italics in the same way.

Clear Formatting

If you change your mind about text you have already formatted, simply do the following:

1. Select the desired text.
2. Click on the Clear Formatting button.

This will erase any formatting such as **bold**, underline, or *italics* from the selected text.

Undo Your Last Command

You can undo your last keystrokes by clicking the Undo button. Think of this button as a do-over button. You will find this button located on the Quick Access Toolbar. Use it once and you will be hooked.

Using the Cut, Copy and Paste Feature

You may want to copy text from one location in your notebook to another. Alternatively, you can permanently move text to another section of your notebook. OneNote has a cut, copy and paste feature that allows you to do this in mere seconds.

Copied text is temporarily moved to the Clipboard. Think of the Clipboard as that magical place where data temporarily waits until you decide where to place it. There are several ways to copy and/or move text in OneNote. For example, if you want to copy text do the following:

1. Select the text you want to copy.
2. Click on the Home tab.
3. Click on the Copy button.
4. Place your mouse where you want the copied text to appear.
5. Click on the Paste button.

Alternatively, you can highlight the selected text, and then use the short-cut keystroke, Ctrl + C to copy. Press Ctrl + V to paste the text where you it to appear.

To Remove or Cut Text

1. Select the text you want to cut.
2. Click on the Cut (scissor icon).

Save Time with Format Painter

If you have worked with Microsoft Word, then you already know what a time-saver the Format Painter can be. This feature allows you to copy the character formatting of a word and then apply it to another word, sentence or paragraph.

To Use the Format Painter

1. Click on the Home tab.
2. Select the word that contains the desired formatting.
3. Click on the Format Painter to copy the formatting.
4. Select the text to be formatted.

Apply a New Font

1. Click on the Home tab.

2. Select the desired text to be formatted.

3. Click on the Font dropdown box and choose the desired font.

4. Click on the Font Size button if you also wish to change the size of the text.

Figure 91

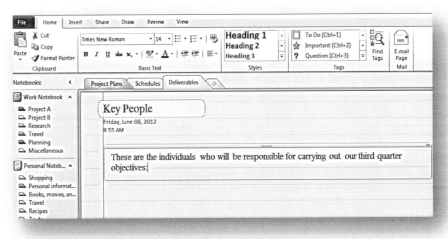

Apply Styles to Basic Text and Save Time

If you are interested in saving some time on formatting your text, consider using the Styles feature. Anyone who has worked with Microsoft Word is likely to be familiar with how to use styles, but if you are a novice, take heart. Think of styles as preformatting. For example, look at the Styles group located on the Home tab.

See Figure 91. The style **Heading 1** is made up of the Calibri Font is **bold** and has a 17-point font size. Using Styles can save you the steps it normally takes to select a font, a character format and font size.

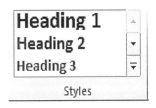

To Apply a Heading Style

1. Click on the Home tab.

2. Select the desired text.

3. Click on the desired heading style.

Spell Checking with OneNote

Microsoft OneNote contains a spelling feature that will automatically check your document for common spelling errors. In addition, you can quickly spell check a word by selecting it, and then clicking on the Spelling button. Be advised that proper nouns and words typed in all capitals are generally **not** reviewed by the Spelling feature.

1. Click on the OneNote Review tab, and then click on the Spelling button.

2. To accept a suggested correction, click the Change button.

If unique words appear in your notebook that you do not wish to have the Spelling program flag, click on the Add to Dictionary button.

Figure 92

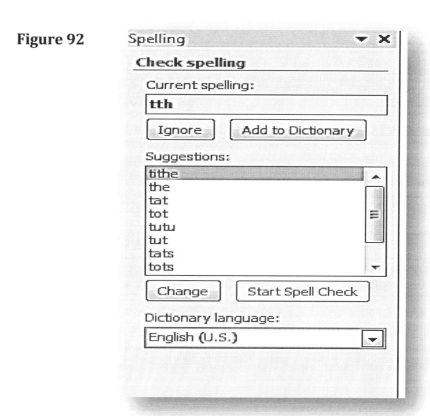

If you are familiar with the spelling and grammar feature in Microsoft's Word, Excel and PowerPoint applications, be advised that OneNote does not include a grammar-checking program. Unlike in Word and Excel, you will also not find a Thesaurus.

Printing Notebook Pages

If you have worked with other applications such as Word or Excel, you may find the print option in OneNote, a bit unfamiliar. Keep in mind that when you choose the Print option from the File tab, all of your existing notebooks will appear on the backstage menu. You must first select the notebook you wish to print, and then choose Print Preview.

When the Print Preview and Settings dialog box opens, you will have the opportunity to select the print range, letter size and orientation. Examine the Print Preview window in Figure 93. From this dialog box, you can also choose to place footer within your printed notebook page.

Figure 93

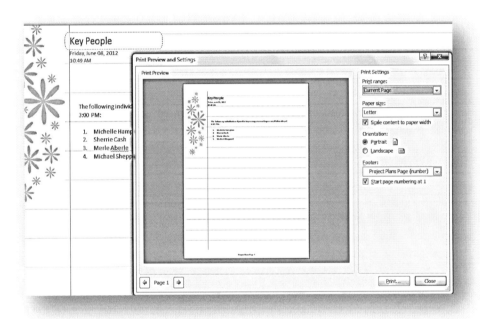

To Print in OneNote

1. Click on the File tab.
2. Click on the Notebook you wish to print.
3. Choose the Print Preview button.
4. Select the print range.
5. Click on the Print button.

Chapter 20

TAGS, FILES & NOTES

- *Create a Tag*

- *Attach Files*

- *Print-out Files*

- *Create Side Notes*

🕐 *The Estimated Time to Complete These Tasks is 9 Minutes.*

Tags for Task Management – Open Tags group
Dropdown box

Figure 94

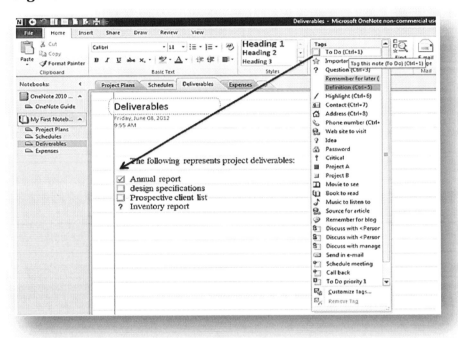

Organization is one of the cornerstones of the OneNote application. OneNote's Tags feature enables you to mark, prioritize, and categorize tasks by tagging your notes. See Figure 94. Notice the tags adjacent to the "Prepare annual report" item. You can quickly mark items as "Important" or place question tags in your notebook text. In fact, there are more than 20 different tags available. In addition, OneNote also enables you to create your own customized tags.

Place Tags in a Notebook Page

1. Click on the Home tab.

2. Place your cursor where you want the tag to appear.

3. Click on the Tags group dropdown box.

4. Choose the desired tag.

Note: To remove a tag, point to the tag, right click your mouse button and select Remove Tag.

Attaching Files to Notebook Pages

One of the coolest features within OneNote is Attach File. This feature enables you to place a copy of a file located on your computer (document, music, etc.,) within any one of your notebook pages.

Figure 95

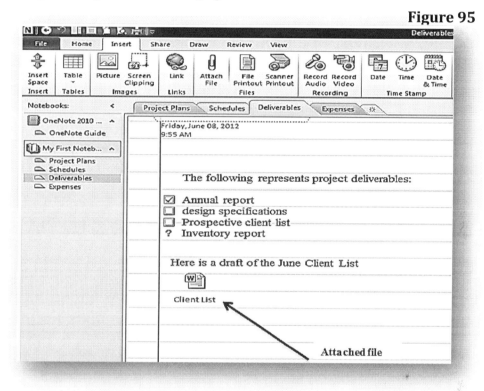

To Attach a File to a Notebook Page

1. Click on the Insert tab.
2. Place your cursor where you want the attached file to appear.
3. Click on the Attach File button.
4. Locate the desired file.
5. Click on the Insert button.

To Use File Printout

1. Click on the Insert tab.
2. Place your cursor where you want the printed file to appear.
3. Click on the File Printout button.
4. Locate the desired file.
5. Click on the Insert button.

Printing Text from External Applications

If you have information stored in other applications, such as Microsoft Word, Excel, PowerPoint or Access, you will be pleased to learn that you can save and print that information to your notebook. For example, assume you wish to print an Excel workbook. When you choose the Printer dropdown box, a list of printers appears. Notice that one print option is to print the document to OneNote 2010.

Figure 96

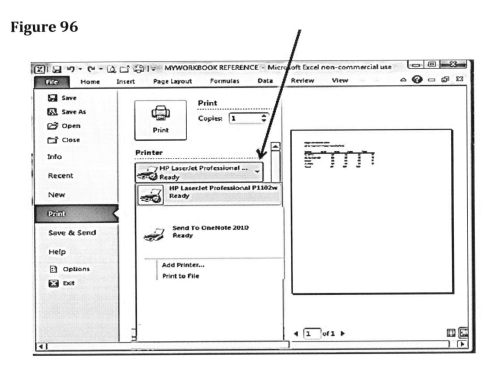

To Print a File to OneNote

1. Open the desired file.

2. Click on the File tab.

3. Choose the Print option.

4. Click on the Printer dropdown box, as though you are choosing another printer.

5. Select the Send to OneNote 2010 option. Continued on the next page☞

After you select the Print button, the Select Location in OneNote dialog box will open. The OneNote application will prompt you to identify where you want your text to appear. See Figure 97 below.

To Select a Location in OneNote

1. Click into the Location field.
2. Select the page in which you want to place your document from All Notebooks.
3. Choose the OK button.

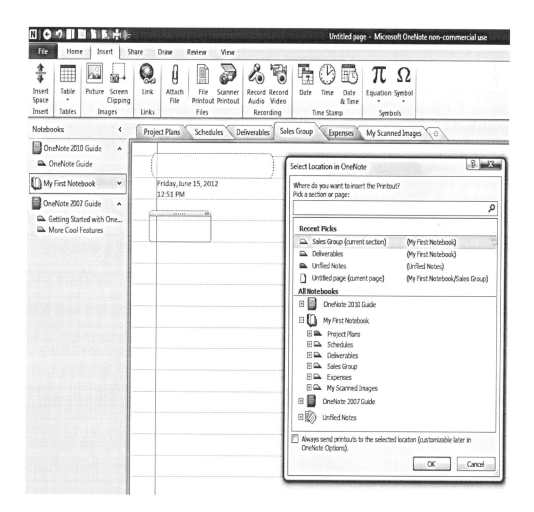

Figure 97

Bring Sticky Notes to Life with a Side Note

If you have ever used those popular little sticky notes as temporary reminders, you will genuinely appreciate Side Note. This feature will enable you to create temporary notes that you can keep open on your desktop. See Figure 98.

Figure 98

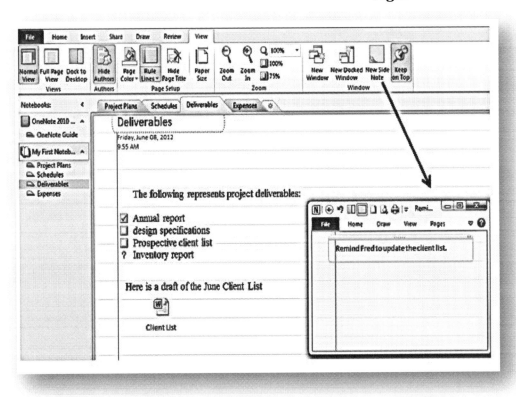

To Create a New Side Note

1. Click on the View tab.

2. Place your cursor anywhere within your notebook.

3. Click on the New Side Note button located within the Window group.

4. Type your note.

To anchor your side note, click on the Keep on Top button, also located within the Window group of the View ribbon.

Chapter 21

TABLES & IMAGES

- *Create a Table*

- *Insert a Picture into a Notebook*

- *Adjust Picture Size*

- *Insert Scanned Images*

- *Use Drawing Tools*

- *Insert Shapes*

The Estimated Time to Complete These Tasks is <u>13</u> Minutes.

Creating Tables in OneNote

Tables can enhance your ability to organize text, and fortunately, they are very easy to create with OneNote. If you have worked with tables in Microsoft Word or PowerPoint, you will recognize OneNote's basic table functions. However, before you decide to skip this section, you should know that Tables in OneNote lack the elegance and full functionality available in Word. For example, there is no table design gallery in OneNote. The differences may take a little getting used to, but it is worth it to spend a little time reviewing the OneNote version.

Figure 99

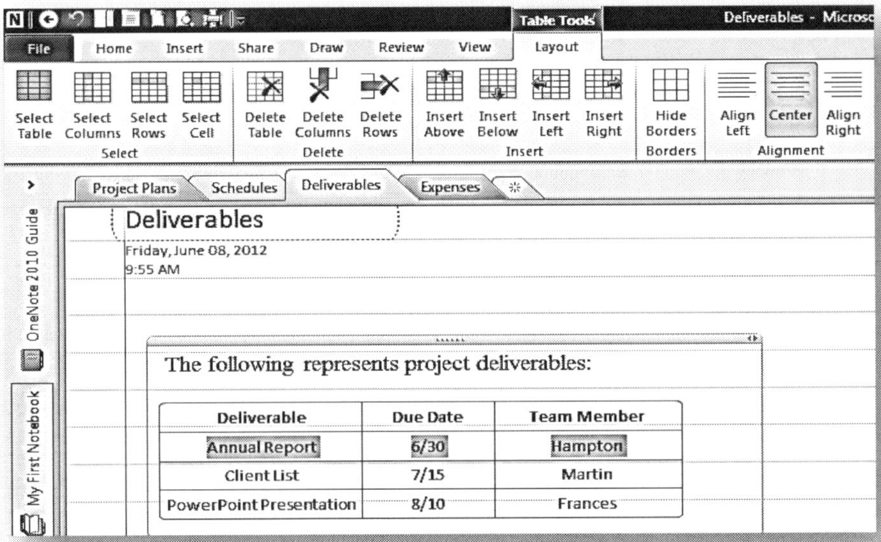

Familiar table options include Select Table, Insert Column and Row Above as well as text alignment buttons, such as Left, Center, Right and Justify. The Table Tools tab appears after you have inserted a table into your notebook. See Figure 99.

To Insert a Table

1. Click on the page where you want the table to appear.

2. Choose the View tab.

3. Click on the Insert Table button.

4. Choose the desired number of columns and rows.

5. Click on the OK button.

Inserting a Picture into a Notebook Page

Pictures can be easily inserted into your notebook with OneNote's Insert Picture feature. When you click on the Insert Picture button, OneNote will enable you to select a picture from any location on your computer.

Figure 100

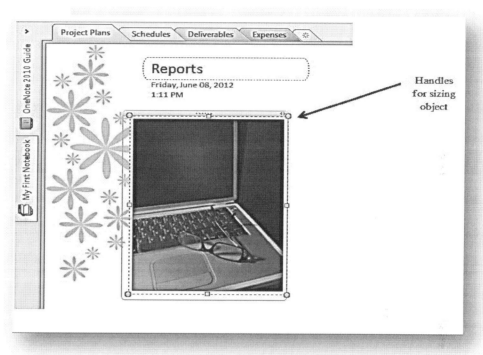

Adjust the Size of Your Picture

After you select your photograph or clip art, OneNote places it into your document surrounded by handles. See Figure 100.

To make an image larger or smaller, simply hover with your mouse over any of the handles, and notice the double arrow. When the double arrow appears, hold down your left mouse button to size the image.

****

Inserting and Managing Scanned Images

Another one of OneNote's best features is Scanner Printout. If you have paper documents that you want to preserve in digital form, you will find it relatively easy to scan them into your Notebook. When you click on the Scanner Printout button, OneNote will automatically communicate with your scanner and place the document into your Notebook. In the graphic below, we have scanned a page from Microsoft's OneNote Tutorial. Of course, to make this work you must have a scanner.

Figure 101

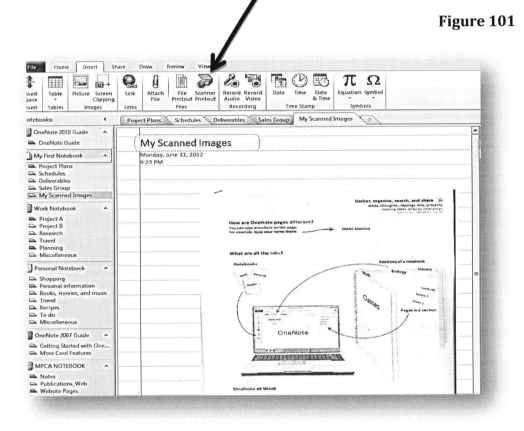

To Scan Documents

1. Place the document on your scanner
2. Click into the page where you want the scanned image to appear.
3. Select the Insert tab.
4. Click the Scanner Printout button.

Working with OneNote's Drawing Tools

You can highlight or mark-up text within your notebook using OneNote's Drawing tools. Click on the Draw tab to view the Tools group. There are more than 30 marker size and/or color options from which to choose. For example, notice how we highlighted the June numbers displayed in Figure 102.

1. Click on the yellow highlighter button then select the desired text

2. Press the Select & Type button to turn off highlighting.

Figure 102

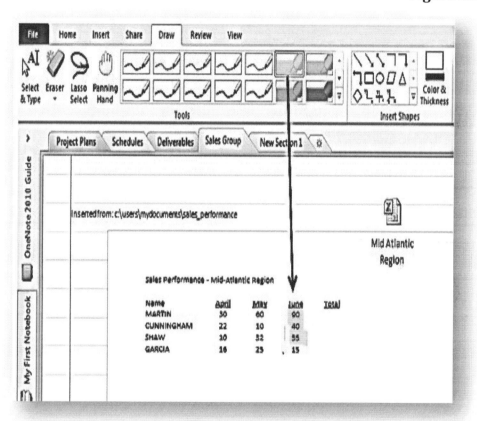

You can erase marked or highlighted text by using the Eraser tool located at the top left hand side of the Tools group. See Figure 102.

1. Click on the Eraser tool.

2. Drag your mouse across the highlighted text.

3. Press the Select & Type button to turn off the Eraser.

Shape Up with the Insert Shapes Button

OneNote's Insert Shapes feature is still impressive though not as extensive as that found in Microsoft Word. With this feature, you can quickly insert basic shapes within your notebook and add color as well. You will find the Insert Shapes button located within the ribbon of the Draw tab. See Figure 103.

Insert a Shape

1. Click on the Draw tab.

2. Select the page where you want to place the shape.

3. Click on the desired shape within the Insert Shapes group.

4. As soon as the cursor turns into a cross hair, drag your mouse to draw the shape.

Figure 103

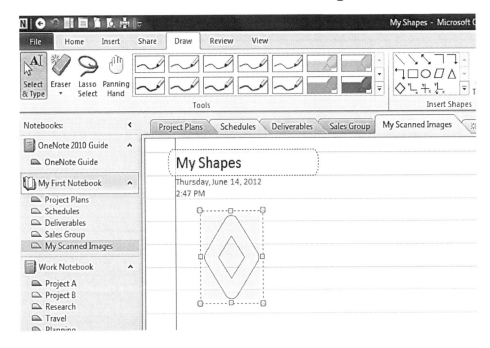

Notice the graphic above has handles. Remember, this means that you can size the shape, making it larger or smaller.

To delete a shape, select it, and when the handles appear, press the delete key.

Chapter 22

COLLABORATION TOOLS

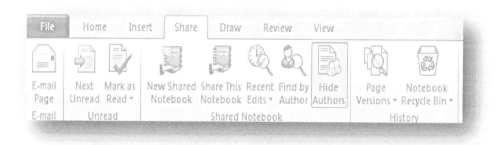

- *Identify Collaboration Tools in OneNote*

- *E-mail a Notebook Page*

- *Identify Shared Notebook Features*

E-Mail a Notebook Page

Assume you have created some rather interesting notebook pages. Should you decide to share these pages, you will find one button makes the task very easy to do.

On OneNote's Share tab, you will find a single button within the E-mail group. When you click on the E-mail Page button, OneNote will attempt to e-mail the active page (where your cursor is located) through your personal or business e-mail account. You may find it easier to open your e-mail program before you select the E-mail Page button. Note that your notebook page will be sent as an attached web page.

Shared Notebooks

Though the subject goes a little beyond the scope of this book, I thought it might be useful to explain a little about OneNote's Shared Notebook feature. Essentially, what you are doing through this feature is placing your files on the Web in a way that makes them accessible to others. OneNote makes it possible to share a notebook with friends or colleagues. In addition, you can also track edits made by others to shared notebooks as well as search for edits by other authors. You will find the Shared Notebook button on OneNote's Share tab. In order to share your notebook however, you will require a SharePoint account through your employer or you must obtain a personal Windows Live ID.

For more information regarding this feature, consult the Microsoft website or your system administrator at work.

Figure 104

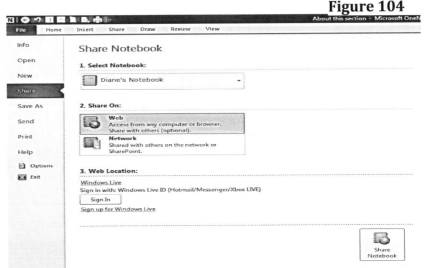

Chapter 23

ONENOTE RIBBONS & TABS

- *File Tab*

- *Home Tab*

- *Insert Tab*

- *Share Tab*

- *Drawing Tab*

- *Review Tab*

- *View Tab*

OneNote Ribbons & Tabs

The File Tab and Backstage View

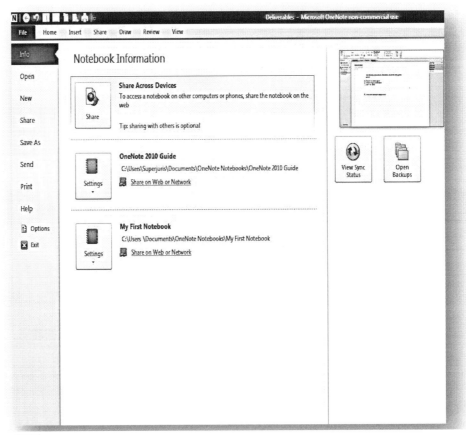

Figure 105

On the File tab, you will find a variety of menu options, such as Info, Open, Save As and Print. You can also exit from OneNote by using this menu.

Additionally, you will find online Help. If you need more information regarding a OneNote feature or function, you will find the online Help system very useful. Choose Options, if you want to customize the OneNote environment. For example, you can customize your ribbons, Autocorrect entries, and display preferences from the Options menu.

From the File tab, you may elect to share your notebook with others within your organization or externally.

OneNote Ribbons & Tabs

Home

On this ribbon, you will find useful tools for managing your notebook content. Notice the groups that reside on this ribbon such as Clipboard, Basic Text, Tags and Mail. You can use E-Mail Page to transmit a page of your notebook to friends or colleagues. You can place a To Do tag within your notes to create a useful checkbox for task management.

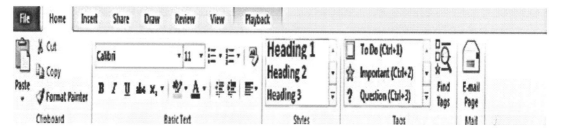

Insert

From the Insert tab, you can place within your notebook everything from a table to a video. Use the objects here to insert audio, video, photographs or recordings into your OneNote pages. In addition, scanned and website images may also be inserted into your notebook.

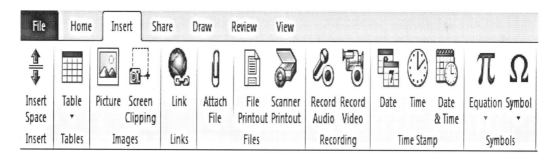

Share

Through OneNote, it is possible to collaborate and share your notebook with others. Create shared notebooks, e-mail specific pages, and track revisions. Here you can also delete old notebooks with the Notebook Recycle Bin.

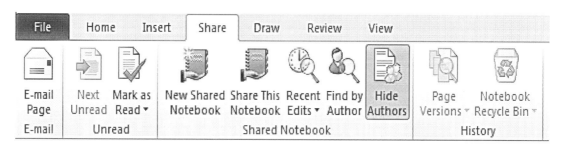

Drawing

Do you like to doodle in your notebook? On this ribbon, you will find a variety of free-hand drawing tools at your disposal. You can highlight text in your notebook just as you would do in hardcopy with OneNote's highlighter pens. You can also insert and color shapes.

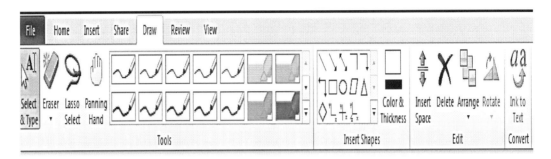

Review

OneNote makes it possible for you to not only create and edit, you can also check your spelling, do quick research of a subject on the Web or link notes in one notebook to another.

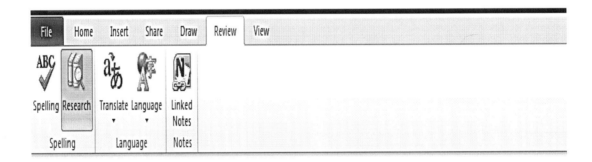

View

You can use the objects on this tab for zooming in and out of text. Enhance your notebook by applying rule lines to the page. In addition, you can change the color of your notebook pages and create side notes as temporary reminders.

Online Resources

You will find a variety of helpful resources on the Internet to assist you with Microsoft PowerPoint; below are just a few.

www.microsoft.com	➢ *Access templates, tutorials and the latest updates concerning Microsoft Office applications and products.*
www.certiport.com	➢ *Use this portal to obtain information on how to become a certified Microsoft Office Specialist.*
www.mypcassociate.com	➢ *Obtain quick reference cards for Excel, Word, Outlook and PowerPoint. Find out about how you can learn new Microsoft applications.*
www.pcworld.com	➢ *Keep up to date with the latest software and hardware products on the market.*
http://www.pcmag.com/	➢ *Check out the PC Magazine web site for the latest news, downloads, deals and product reviews.*
http://magazine-directory.com/Smart-Computing.htm	➢ *Smart Computing is another great web site if you want to keep abreast of what is going on in the land of computers.*

My Notes:

My Notes:

My Notes:

Index

A

Absolute cell references, 58
Add content, (OneNote), 126
Add new slides, 77
Alignment group buttons (Excel) 53
Aligning text (Word), 9
Animations, 108
Applying styles, Word 11
Attach files, (OneNote) 143
AutoSum, (Excel) 39
Average, 41

B

Backstage view (Word), 34
Bulleted text (PowerPoint) 74
Bullets & Numbering, 10

C

Character formatting, 8
Charts, embedded, 60
Clear cell contents, 51
Clear formatting, (Word) 11
Clip art gallery, (Word) 24
Close a document, 4
Close a workbook, 42
Copying formulas, 58
Create a new document, 6
Create sections OneNote, 132
Cut, copy and paste text, 16

D

Data tab, 72
Delete cell contents, 51

D (continued)

Design tab, (PowerPoint) 119
Design themes, (PowerPoint) 83
Developer tab, (Excel) 72
Drawing tools, 150

E

E-mail a notebook page, 54

F

Fill series, 57
File tab, (Excel) 70
File tab, (PowerPoint) 118
File tab, (Word) 34
Fonts, change, 8
Format cells, 50
Format painter, 9
Format tab, (PowerPoint) 121
Formulas tab, 71
Footers, (Excel) 45
Footers, (PowerPoint), 85
Footers, (Word) 13

H

Headers, (Word) 12
Home tab, (Excel) 71
Home tab, (Word) 1-35

I

Insert columns, (Excel) 52
Insert rows, 52

Transitions, slides, 109

U

Undo command, 11

V

View multiple presentations, 79
View tab, (Word) 36

W

Worksheet, entering data, 40

Z

Zoom control, 2

24574534R00099